MICHAEL DURACK

Conversations
WITH A Deaf Cat

20 Twenty
Literary Group

Conversations with a Deaf Cat
Copyright © 2025 by Michael Durack

ISBN
978-1-962868-25-9 (Paperback)
978-1-962868-26-6 (eBook)
978-1-964488-48-6 (Hardcover)

CONVERSATIONS
WITH A DEAF CAT

TABLE OF CONTENTS

FOREWORD

The cat's name was Kwartel. She was born deaf, and just like Americans have a saying "deaf as doorknob", the Dutch have a saying "zo doof als een kwartel", which means basically the same thing. Kwartel was a beautiful snow white cat, but she was also the skinniest cat I ever saw. My wife, Yolande, told me she had a thyroid problem which made her constantly hungry, but even though she ate like crazy, she never gained any weight. So my job was to feed her whenever she came around meowing, which was something like 5 or 6 times a day. I didn't really mind, even though her hunger pangs sometimes hit her at four or five in the morning, because I could talk to her and pretend she understood me, even though she was a Dutch cat that couldn't hear and I could only speak English. No one else in the household spoke much, if any English, except Yolande and she was usually almost totally absorbed by the strain of caring for her mother, so the cat seemed to be a willing listener. In any event, we were the only two creatures awake in the house at these times, so it seemed to make sense.

Yolande and I were living with my in-laws in Holland as personal caregivers for my mother-in-law, who was battling ALS disease. We had just left our most recent assignment as volunteers for a First Nations group in Canada, and were beginning to wonder just how much good we were actually doing. Yolande's mother definitely needed in-home care since the disease was slowly robbing her of her ability to perform basic functions. Since I didn't speak Dutch however, Yolande was forced to deal with the brunt of the caretaking duties, and it was obvious they were desperately needed. The problem was that, despite her illness, her mother didn't really want our help, whether she needed it or not. As a result, my wife was involved in countless arguments with her mother every day in an ongoing battle to try to help her cope with her illness. Although it was definitely frustrating and depressing for us, we both understood that it was so much worse for her.

While we dealt with the challenge of caring for her while she fought what everyone knew would be a losing battle, we pondered what the next step in our odyssey as foreign teachers and/or volunteers would be after its inevitable conclusion. We had already spent four months in China and a year in Chile as foreign teachers, as well as a three-month stint in Canada before undertaking our caretaking duties and felt we had learned how to spot the pitfalls associated with foreign teaching or volunteer assignments. Although it might seem callous to be worrying about such things while caring for a loved one with a terminal disease, it was often one of the very few things we could look forward to in the midst of our grim daily routine.

I heard Kwartel meowing at three in the morning. I got up off the mattress which lay on the floor next to my wife's mattress and pulled on a pair of pants before I walked out into the hall. Our tiny bedroom lay directly across the hall from my mother in law's room, and no matter what time I rose to feed Kwartel, she was always awake, staring at me as I walked out into the hallway. Sometimes she would attempt to talk, but since I barely spoke Dutch and she barely spoke English, she usually just watched me silently.

Tonight was no different as I opened the door and smiled at her. I also gave her a feeble wave, which seemed totally out of place, but I never knew what else to do. She never smiled when

I did this. I imagined I wouldn't feel much like smiling either, but she gave me a nod, or as much of a nod as she could manage. Sometimes it was barely perceptible, but I could tell she was trying to acknowledge me.

I walked to the end of the hall and opened the door. Kwartel was standing there, waiting for me. She let out another loud meow when she saw me, as if she wanted to ask what the hell kept me so long. I went into the kitchen and spooned out her cat food into her bowl and watched as she wolfed it down. She obviously was ravenous, so I forgave her for waking me up again at such an ungodly hour.

Since I was now wide awake and I knew it would take some time for me to fall asleep again, I poured myself a Dutch beer and sat down at the dining room table in the next room. I took a few sips before I noticed Kwartel had already finished her meal and was sitting next to my feet, watching me.

"Feel better now, Kwartel?" I asked her.

Kwartel just looked at me. She appeared to know I was talking, and I wondered if that seemed as ridiculous to her as it did to me. However, at that point talking to a deaf cat seemed no more ridiculous than the adventures Yolande and I had taken over the past few years as part of our foreign teaching experiences. Besides, sitting there and speaking to the cat (or "de poes" as they say in Dutch) somehow helped me make sense out of why Yolande and I had decided to become volunteer teachers three years before. I was hoping it would also help me decide if it was something we wanted to continue or not. Lord knows there had been almost as many ups as there were downs. Still, there was something about going to a new country and experiencing a new culture that seemed almost irresistible.

"What should we do next, Kwartel?"

Kwartel continued staring at me, knowing full well that I didn't really want her to answer, even if she could.

"It hasn't gone exactly the way we planned it, has it?" She continued to stare at me, blinking every minute or so.

"Still, you have to admit, it's been *different!*" I said. Still no response from the cat, so I continued with my soliloquy. "How did it all begin, you ask? Well, I'm glad you seem so interested" I told her.

"Well, I guess we should start at the beginning. It all began with China…

China

"China is totally modern now! We even have McDonalds!"

Ernie Chang was talking to me on Skype from a fast-food coffee shop in China. He held up the styrofoam cup he was drinking from to show me what a modern place I would be traveling to within a few days.

I pointed out to him that the cup he was showing me had "Caribou Coffee" printed on it instead of McDonald's, but he dismissed the comment, saying "Ahh! McDonald's! Caribou! What's the difference?"

Well there was a difference, obviously, but at that point it was totally irrelevant as far as I or anyone else was concerned. I was going to be in China working as a foreign English teacher within a week or so, and I wasn't overly concerned about what type of fast-food restaurants or coffee shops were available there. But there would come a time when I would thank heaven if I could find a McDonald's *anywhere* in China. The food there was definitely an experience, and usually not the kind I wanted.

But I'm starting to get ahead of myself. How did I get to this point, you ask? Well, let me tell you….

It all started with my annual performance review for the company I worked for in Long Beach.

****

It wasn't working.

There were a lot of reasons and personality conflicts that all went into it, but I won't bore you with the details. The fact is that I had worked in a management position for a company in Long Beach for over three years, and it had slowly evolved into a situation that wasn't satisfactory to me or to my boss. Furthermore, what once had been a friendly relationship between the two of us had changed as a result of philosophical differences related to management policies, combined with some finger pointing about who was to blame for a couple of significant problems in my department. I could give you a truckload of details to try to sway you to my point of view, but why bother? The fact was that I had received an annual review of my performance which I felt was unfair and shortly afterwards I gave my boss my letter of resignation.

This came as a bit of a shock to him and he suggested we have a meeting in a public place along with our company's Human Resources manager to air our differences. We did this at a local restaurant, but it didn't resolve anything. If anything, it probably made both of us more certain that we were right and he (thr opponent) was wrong. And after working in the corporate world for over 30 years, I wasn't ready to back down from what I felt was an attempt to paint me as a scapegoat. I was really getting tired of the corporate rat race routine anyway. After a few more meetings that didn't actually change anything, we both agreed that it was in everyone's best interests for me to move on.

But move on to what? I searched around on the internet for a few days looking for something along the lines of *Training* or *Teaching*, since I didn't want to get stuck in a strictly accounting job again, and one day I stumbled onto teaching EFL, aka *English as a Foreign Language*.

This sounded interesting. It looked like there were opportunities to teach in other countries all over the world if you had something called a TEFL or a TESOL or a CELTA certificate, or some combination of all three. I later found out that these acronyms stood for *Teaching English as a Foreign Language, Teaching English as a Second Occupational Language* and *Certificate in English Language Training to Adults.*

I decided this might be worth looking into a little further. I found out that, like anything else, the type of certificate you wanted depended a lot on how much time you were willing to spend to get it, and how much you were willing to pay. I checked out a few of the TEFL/TESOL/CELTA training programs and found one that was based in Los Angeles that didn't cost an arm and a leg and could be done partially via the internet.

Cut to two months later and I had completed all of my on line and in-class training so that I now had my 120 hour TEFL certificate. Now I just had to find a position where I could use it and where Yolande could also get some type of job to keep her busy. There were several possibilities, but the one that seemed the best fit was an organization that offered both of us a chance to teach - in China!

Now, up until a few years earlier, I would have told anyone who suggested I move to China to teach English that they were ready for the Funny Farm. I didn't speak the language, I was concerned about the fact that it was a Communist country that didn't observe the same basic human rights or customs that we had in America, and that teaching English was something I had never done before. But after talking it over with my wife, and considering the alternative of once more looking for a routine, insecure corporate job, we both decided it was time for a change – and this would definitely be a big one.

So now it was time to put my money where my mouth was. Did I really want to take a chance and leave the relatively safe and sound borders of the U. S. A. where I was born and raised and lived in for almost all of my life? Or did I want to play it safe and live out the end of my career supervising accounting clerks and preparing financial reports? I thought about it for an hour or so and decided it was finally time to spread my wings and fly. Yolande and I both had a Skype interview with Ernie Chang, our recruiter, and after several more online meetings and getting our travel visas from the Chinese consulate in L.A., we were ready to make our move. Look out, China, here we come!

It didn't come without some hardships and sacrifice, of course. In addition to getting the TEFL certificate, we had the physical challenge of deciding what clothes and personal belongings we wanted to take with us and selling everything else. This included my car, our televisions, all our furniture and a load of books, pictures, knick knacks, souvenirs, etc. The good news is we only had a one-bedroom apartment, so the furniture and everything else that had to go was a lot less than what most people our age would have accumulated. Still, we had to organize and conduct a two-day yard sale in order to get rid of everything we couldn't take with us and hopefully end up with a few dollars for it, just to avoid a total loss. Anything that didn't get sold ended up being donated to a local charity. And of course, we had to say goodbye to family and friends, so we took a final trip to Chicago and Wisconsin to take care of that obligation before we left.

Finally we were ready! We had a 15 hour flight from Los Angeles to Guangzhou and then, after a 2 hour layover, another 3 hour flight before we got to Dalian, where we would have "3 days" of training. I remember sitting in a fast-food restaurant in the international terminal at LAX with Yolande before getting on our plane to Guangzhou and asking her if she really believed this was going to happen. We were about to embark on a journey that even 6 months earlier, neither one of us would have ever thought would happen.

I asked her if we were both basically insane for even attempting such a thing. She laughed and said 'Yeah, but you might as well do something insane rather than work at a job you hate all your life."

That pretty much summarized our philosophy about this trip and the ones which would follow. However, we soon found out that, even though we thought we covered everything we should expect and what would be expected from us from our Skype interviews, we soon found out that the most important parts about teaching abroad are the things that they *don't* tell you!

After we landed in Dalian and retrieved our luggage, the first hint we had that the Chinese agency we were dealing with weren't as prepared for us as we had thought was when we saw the car they sent to pick us up.

It was a Chinese car of some sort, with an inside space about as large as you would find in a standard VW Beetle. The only problem was there were two people from the agency, and the two of us – but we had *luggage*!

I didn't think we brought an excessive amount of luggage, considering we were planning on being there a full year, but apparently our Chinese recruiting agency friends must have thought we were going to make the trip from L.A. with just a couple of carry-on bags. There was no room whatsoever in the car they sent for us for *any* amount of luggage, much less the two extra-large suitcases, two large backpacks and two carry-on bags we brought.

Our female liaison, Ellen, (We'll call her Ellen. I forget her real name.) took one look at the luggage we had on our cart when we emerged from the baggage claim area and muttered something in Chinese that we didn't understand, but knew it had to be something along the lines of "Oh, My God!"

After a few minutes, she and the driver realized there was absolutely no way the four of us were ever going to fit in that car with our luggage, so they proposed a different approach. The driver would load the luggage into the car and take it to our hotel where we would stay for a few days, and Ellen, Yolande and I would have to take public transportation.

It actually worked out fairly well, although I was surprised they hadn't considered that we would have more luggage than most people would need for a week or so. After all, our contract was supposed to be for a full year. A similar situation occurred when I asked Ellen how I could exchange some American money for Chinese currency. I had been told this particular agency had been doing this for something like 18 years, so I had assumed they had some procedure in place to provide newcomers with the local currency. However, Ellen didn't seem to have any idea as to how we would go about doing this, so we walked to 3 or 4 ATMS before we found one that I could use my American bank card in to withdraw some local cash.

The biggest surprise came about on the day we actually started teaching, however.

We had been promised 3 days of training in Dalian before we transferred to Shenyang, the city where we would actually be teaching and living. The 3 days turned out to be more like only 2 hours of training. The rest of the time we were in Dalian we were given some sample teaching materials and chauffeured back and forth to a local hospital where we were examined by Chinese doctors to make sure we didn't have any diseases to infect the school kids with.

Even with this minimal amount of training, we felt like we were ready to give the real thing a try. The next day, we took a train from Dalian to Shenyang, had dinner with our recruiter, teaching assistants and the principal of the school we would be teaching at, and showed up at the school the next morning to start our teaching careers.

Although the school we came to on the first day was one in which Yolande would be teaching, I had been assigned to two other schools farther away from the city center. However, for purposes of our training, we were both supposed to teach our classes together for the first day.

Nobody had told us exactly how we were supposed to do this, so Yolande and I decided on our own as to which basic subject she would be teaching and which one I would teach. Keep in mind that the students we were teaching were basically kindergarten aged kids, around 3 to 4 years old. Although I had been told I would be teaching adults and adolescents to prepare them for an IELTS exam, which was an English exam students must pass if they wish to study or work in America, Canada or Europe, we had been told after I arrived, that the IELTS class was not ready yet, so I would be teaching kindergarten aged kids temporarily. I didn't mind that as long as it wasn't a permanent situation, and Ernie, our recruiter had assured me it wouldn't be.

So, here we were on the first day of class, in front of a room of about twenty 4-year old kids, a couple of Chinese teachers and an "observer" named Mary, who had been present during our 2 hour training session. Yolande covered one subject, which involved presenting a few basic words along with some pictures to reinforce their meaning. Now it was my turn, and I walked up to the whiteboard to erase what Yolande had written so that I could start to teach the lesson I had prepared.

I got halfway through erasing the whiteboard when Mary came up to me in front of the class and whispered "Michael, what are you doing?"

I looked at her in amazement. "I'm going to teach the next vocabulary section", I said.

"You cannot do that now. Yolande started teaching the class. She is the only one who is supposed to teach today!"

"But Ernie told me yesterday that both of us were supposed to teach on a trial basis today", I countered.

"Yes, but only Yolande can teach. You must just watch for today".

I looked over at Yolande and for a moment, I thought she was just going to throw down her markers and walk out. This was not what we had been told, and we never expected to have our teaching interfered with in front of the students we were teaching. However, we were in China now, so we figured it might be better to do what they wanted us to do and complain to our recruiter later.

I did call him to complain that night and he assured me that it was just a big misunderstanding. Apparently, in China, people do not allow more than one person to teach any one class, so my trying to jump in and teach part of a lesson that Yolande had already started was looked upon as a big "no-no". Unfortunately, that was just the beginning.

We ultimately had several other misunderstandings during our stay in China. Another memorable one occurred when we rented an apartment with our agency's help.

Shenyang was a very big city by American standards, but to the Chinese it was just a small town of over 8,000,000 people. In other words, their "small towns" were about the size of New York City!

Our Chinese assistant who would help us find an apartment was a young, very friendly Chinese woman who called herself "Sky". The Chinese assistants liked to give themselves catchy English names, so in addition to "Sky", the agency had an assistant named "Smile", who would become Yolande's personal assistant and one named "Lollipop", who became my personal assistant. Sky's first order of business was to show us around to five different apartments in the city and help us decide which one we wanted and negotiate the monthly rent.

We looked at four different units the first weekend afternoon. They all seemed pretty similar in terms of space, differing only in the layout. We finally decided to rent a brand new apartment in a high-rise building on a promenade inside a shopping mall and literally steps away from the city's only subway line. The main reason we chose it was for the close transportation options of bus or subway train, but the agency staff thought we had decided on it because it was the most expensive unit we were shown. They teased us about having a "luxury apartment" and paying a fortune in monthly rent. Since it only cost the equivalent of $400 per month in American money, we really didn't think it was all that expensive. In any event, it seemed like the best option available, so we told the Chinese lady who was showing it that we would take it.

The next day we had to move our luggage from the hotel we had stayed in for the first three days to our new apartment. In order to do this, we had to split up into two vehicles. I went ahead with a taxi and the luggage that would fit inside the back seat and trunk, but Yolande and Sky had to hire a man on a bicycle pushing a cart which was large enough to carry one of our large suitcases and a few smaller ones. Yolande and Sky also had to sit inside the cart, but the weather was still very warm, so it wasn't any big deal.

Now, if you think the traffic is bad in the U.S., you don't know what *really* bad traffic is until you come to China. Every street seems to be a bottleneck of cars that are stuck in bumper-to-bumper traffic jams until something magical happens and they can start to move. And then, it seems like the drivers think that the more they honk their horns, the faster the traffic will go. So, shortly after hailing a taxi and having Sky tell the driver where I had to go, I got in the front seat on the passenger's side and we started the slow, grinding trip to my new apartment.

The traffic was indescribably slow, and my driver must have been working an extremely long shift because he definitely needed some sleep. I found this out the first time we came to a stop and he promptly fell asleep. When the traffic started moving again, I had to shake him to wake him up. This performance kept repeating itself over and over while we drove to the apartment. Every time we came to a stop, his head would drop back and he would immediately become unconscious. Then, when the traffic started moving and the horns started blaring, I'd have to shake him to wake him up again. This went on every four or five minutes for over an hour while we plodded along the traffic choked street.

After about an hour and 15 minutes we made it to the mall my apartment was in. I got out of the cab, got my luggage and paid the driver by showing him the Chinese money I had and asking him to take what he needed. Not the best method to use when it came to payments in China, I know, but without being able to speak the language, I didn't feel I had much of a choice. Besides I knew I was running very late and I had to get to the apartment where I was sure Yolande and Sky would be waiting.

I piled my carry-on bag on top of my big rolling suitcase and walked into the small plaza between stores and high-rise buildings on the block where our building was located. I looked around for Sky and Yolande, but I didn't see them anywhere. It was now almost noon, and our appointment to meet with our landlady and pay our security deposit and first and last month's rent had been set for ten thirty. I got into the elevator and started preparing my apology to Yo and Sky as I headed for the twenty first floor.

When I finally got to the apartment, I found the landlady waiting for me, but no Yo and Sky. I suddenly realized that, even though I was almost an hour and a half late, I had still beaten them to the apartment!

The landlady was a Chinese woman in her early forties who didn't speak much English, but I soon found out she could speak enough to let me know she was not happy about having been kept waiting so long.

"Why you so late?", she yelled at me as I walked through the door.

"I'm sorry, the traffic was terrible!"

"Why you so late?", she yelled at me again, this time even louder.

"I couldn't help it! The taxi couldn't get through the traffic", I tried to explain.

"I come here at ten thirty! You one and a half hours late! You need to get up early!"

I wanted to explain that I didn't set up the time, and that we were just following the instructions Sky had given us about when to leave, but I didn't think she knew enough English to understand. She was so mad that she probably wouldn't care anyway.

The worst part about the whole situation was that I was still the only one there beside the landlady. Sky and Yolande had yet to appear and every minute that went by while we waited for them only made the lady angrier.

"Where your wife? Where your wife?" she asked me several times.

"I don't know. Stuck in traffic, I guess."

"Where your wife?"

After reciting the same answer four or five times, I finally gave up trying to explain. I just started giving her a shoulder shrug with my palms stretched out each time she asked "Where your wife?" Even that didn't stop her for long. She would ask the question, look disgustedly as I tried to mime "I don't know" each time, wait two minutes and then ask me again.

Finally on the sixth or seventh "Where your wife?" Sky and Yolande miraculously walked through the door with the rest of our luggage. The landlady immediately launched into a tirade in Chinese, directed at Sky, since she was the only one who could truly appreciate and understand the tongue lashing she had to endure. After three or four minutes of intense verbal ping pong between the two of them, it appeared the lady was finally ready to give us the lease to sign and get her money.

Sky read the lease agreement in Chinese and then briefly translated the basic terms and how it was a 6-month lease that we would be obligated to pay, even if we left before then, etc., etc. Yo and I basically nodded our heads and said fine, where do we sign. We signed off on the lease and handed over the money to the landlady. For the first time, she started to calm down and started talking to us in English again.

Yolande apologized to her for being late, just like I had, but for some reason, it seemed more acceptable to the landlady when it came from her. She then actually started asking us what we were doing in China and when we told her we were teaching English, she told us her son was learning English in his school. Slowly but surely, as Yo kept on chatting with her, she actually seemed to warm up to both of us. She told us her husband bought the apartment as an investment, no one had lived there before, and he would be able to connect the gas "stove" (more like two burners connected with tubing on a counter top) once they were able to turn on the gas for the building. Obviously we were two of the first new tenants in the building.

Despite being so upset about being kept waiting, the landlady hung around for about another half hour, chatting with Yo and

Sky and trying to practice her English. Naturally, we told her it was very good, much better than our Chinese anyway, and this seemed to make her very happy. She finally left and told us, through Sky, to contact her if we had any problems and she would send her husband over to fix any problems we had.

I told Yo about the brow beating I had to endure for the half hour it took them to arrive and she was surprisingly rather indignant about it. "It's a good thing she didn't say all that to me", Yo said. "I was so fed up with the traffic by the time we got here, I would've turned around said let's just forget the whole thing and go back to America!"

I was really surprised to hear her talk this way. *I was supposed to be the impatient one.* She was the one who would always give people the benefit of the doubt and try to understand what kind of problems they were having if they were hostile or unpleasant in any way. It seemed like the Shenyang traffic had already started to change her attitude about things like this. As we would soon find out, this would not be the last time.

Ernie Chang seemed like a really nice guy during our Skype interviews while were still in the U.S., and after meeting him we still thought he was a really nice guy. His parents were from China, but he grew up in Calgary in Alberta, Canada. As a result, he had learned both Mandarin and English from a very young age. Even better, he understood Canadian customs and slang, which was almost identical to the American customs and slang I learned growing up. He could switch from one language to another in a heartbeat and was extremely friendly and helpful after we first arrived in China.

He arranged a welcome dinner with the principal of the school where Yolande would be teaching and Madame Zhou, the office manager for the Shenyang branch office of the agency we were recruited by. Everyone was very cordial and we were treated to an expensive meal at one of the most expensive restaurants in Shenyang.

The next weekend we were both invited to the grand opening of the school where Yolande would be teaching. Although she had already taught classes there during our first day of "classroom training" and the day after, this was the "official" opening and the local school officials made sure it was an impressive event.

When we arrived, the school was decorated with banners and balloons and there was a stage set up in the courtyard in front of the school with several rows of chairs set out in front for spectators. At the entrance of the school, there were at least six young, tall, slim female Chinese models wearing bright red, satiny dresses with their hair and makeup camera ready for a walk down the red carpet at the Academy Awards. Many of the men attending the opening wore suits and ties and most of the women had formal dresses on.

Yolande and I had to pose for pictures with the school principal, Madam Zhou and Sky in front of the main entrance, with two of the models smiling on either side of us. We then took our seats in one of the middle rows of folding chairs when Sky told us the ceremony was almost ready to begin.

We then sat through a parade of students who came on stage with their teachers, one class at a time and performed a song or dance or a combination of the two wearing colorful costumes. The parents in the audience were just as proud and pleased as any parent watching their kid in a school play or ceremony, especially if the kid forgot his or her lines, or was too young to really understand what he or she was supposed to do and ended up wandering off the stage.

As the parade of kids seemed to be nearing an end, Sky stood at the end of our row of chairs and whispered to Yolande to get up and join her. She did so as quickly as she could, trying not to step on anyone's toes as she made her way out of the narrow row and was quickly escorted to the side of the stage. A group of about 6 or 7 men in suits also appeared at the edge of the stage and were led out onto it by one of the models. Then a long, thick pink ribbon was unrolled and another one of the models appeared with a large scissors. Suddenly, I realized Yolande was going to be part of the ribbon cutting ceremony to dedicate the new school!

Before the ribbon cutting could begin, however, every person on the stage was introduced. Sky was sitting next to me and telling me who each person was in English. There was a banker, the mayor, some other type of political or business bigwigs, and then there was Yolande. She got introduced too, as the foreign English teacher who would help the parents' children learn perfect English. On top of that the next name I heard was my own, and according to Sky, I was being introduced as another foreign English teacher who would also be teaching at another school in Shenyang. I smiled and waved to the crowd while they politely applauded, simply because I didn't know what else to do.

Then, to our surprise, one of the models handed the big scissors to Yolande. She was the one who would actually cut the ribbon! She was just as surprised as I was but was able to perform the task without any problem.

After the ceremony ended, we were whisked off to another expensive restaurant for a celebratory luncheon with Sky, Madam Zhou and the other dignitaries who had participated in the ribbon cutting. It was another fancy Chinese feast with many different foods to sample from a lazy susan plate. However, although it was obvious that the luncheon was intended to be a very impressive feast, I have to be honest and say that most of the food was less than delicious, at least to my taste buds. Still, we tried to sample most of the foods we found edible (I couldn't bring myself to eat any of the fish with heads still intact, staring up at me from the plate), in order not to offend our hosts.

At one point a wave of excitement seemed to spread through the room as a young Chinese man with a bald head entered the room. We were told he was a very popular actor in a show on Chinese TV, and were led over to be introduced and shake his hand, along with the other guests who wanted to meet him. A short while later, the same thing happened when another older man appeared. We were told he was a very famous film director and we were once again ushered over to meet him, and this time we had our picture taken with him as well.

None of this helped me pursue any type of acting career in China, however. Once the luncheon was over, we took the bus to the subway and the subway back to our apartment. It seemed like we were going to be treated like rock stars at the schools where we would be teaching.

This started to change quickly once Yolande started teaching at the school on a regular basis. The principal of the school, whom we had met at the welcoming dinner and then at the grand opening ceremony was quite a different person during the work week. She required Yolande and an assistant/ translator to meet with her every morning to discuss what lessons were being taught and how the kids seemed to be progressing, etc. The strange part about it was that the principal would never talk to Yo directly. Instead, she would have long, rambling discussions with the interpreter in Chinese, after which the interpreter would give Yolande a very brief, uninformative summary.

"She says the kids need to learn more words" might be one example.

This would be the only message Yo would get after a 3 or 4 minute conversation between the principal and the interpreter in which Yo would hear her name mentioned several times. This became a very sore point after a while, since Yo knew the principal was saying a lot more than the interpreter was sharing with her, and she could only guess as to why she was not conveying the entire conversation.

Another problem arose when Yo discovered that there would be a mandatory 20-minute period in which she simply had to wait in the principal's office, while the students attended a flag saluting ceremony in front of the school. She did not feel that she had to be spending time at the school for which she would not be paid (we were only paid for the classes we taught), especially when the mandatory patriotic sessions started stretching out to 25, 30 and even 40 minutes at times.

This also caused problems when it came to scheduling the classes. The way our classes were arranged was that we were basically treated as a "guest teacher" who would come into a class in progress and spend a half hour teaching English. Once we were finished, we would move to a different class and interrupt whatever they were working on and repeat the procedure. The problem arose whenever anything took longer than expected, like the mandatory patriotic exercise. Our classes could not go beyond 30 minutes and we had 4 or 5 classes that were supposed to be taught at each school each day, and we could not extend any of the classes if were running late because we both had to teach at a morning school and an afternoon school. Yolande had to leave at a specific time in order to catch the bus and subway she needed to take to get to her afternoon school on time. This didn't seem to concern the morning school principal and although Yolande mentioned it to the translator at her morning meetings, the principal made no effort to change her procedures, and never lowered herself to talk to Yo about it directly.

There would be more problems forthcoming related to interfering with Yo's teaching methods, but one of the most frustrating problems for Yo was simply being ignored by the principal at her morning school.

For me, the problems began even before we arrived in Shenyang, when we met Ernie Chang in the Dalian offices for the first time. That was when I was told that the advanced English proficiency test I had been hired to teach was not yet ready to be launched, and I would have to teach English to *kindergarten aged students* until enough students could be attained to schedule an IELTS (International English Language Testing System) preparation class.

I didn't really mind teaching the kindergarten classes that much. Most of the kids were pretty cute and at least half of them were interested in the lessons I had prepared. It was everything that went with the teaching part, beginning with the transportation.

Both Yolande and I taught our classes at two different schools – she taught at one for about 3 hours in the morning and one for about 2 hours in the afternoon and my teaching schedule was a little less. She could walk to the school where she taught in the morning and then took a bus and the subway to the school where she taught in the afternoon. It took her about ten minutes to walk to her morning school and about 45 minutes to commute to her afternoon school. She taught her classes from Monday to Friday, five days a week. I, on the other hand only taught my classes three days a week – but the commute to the schools I taught at was *pure hell*.

The day before we started teaching our regular classes at both schools, Sky came to the promenade where our apartment building was located and brought our two new assistants with her – Smile and Lollipop. When they introduced themselves, I almost had to bite my tongue when the pretty young twenty something Chinese girl in front of me told me her name was Lollipop! But, I figured, if that's what she wants to be called, who am I to argue?

As part of her orientation with the language school, Lollipop had written a list, in English, of the bus number I had to get on and the number of stops I had to pass until I should get off that bus and transfer to another one to get to the morning school. I was a little surprised when she showed me the list and found out I had to pass 16 stops before I would get off to transfer to the second bus. She didn't have a list of the stops I had to pass or the bus number for the second bus because she assured me she would be waiting at the stop where I would be getting off to transfer to the second bus, and she would guide me to the school from there.

She sounded like she had been pretty thorough in checking out the route, but I was still a little nervous about taking a bus into a part of the city I hadn't been in before by myself. I mean, it might be hard for me to find my way back in a city of 8,000,000 people where I didn't speak their language if I were to get lost. However,

Lollipop assured me she had taken the route herself and counted all the stops and she was positive she had the correct number written down. Furthermore, she assured me she would meet me at the transfer point at 7:00 am the next day. I didn't really have any choice but to trust her.

The next morning, I got up at 5:15 to get dressed and walk down to the bus stop that Lollipop had told me was where I needed to be by 6:00 am to catch the bus I needed to take. I got to the bus stop around 5 minutes before 6:00 and waited for my bus. I started getting nervous when it didn't arrive for another 20 minutes, so I called the language school's office to make sure I had the right bus stop, but of course at 6:10 in the morning, no one was there to answer the phone. Finally the bus arrived at 6:15 and I breathed a short sigh of relief.

Once I was on the bus, I made sure I counted each and every stop. The only way I knew when to get off was when I reached the 17th stop. This was especially important because the buses in China did not follow linear routes, but instead made several turns, right and left, traveling on several different streets, so if I got off at the wrong stop, I couldn't just cross over to the other side of the street and take a bus coming in the opposite direction to return to my starting point. That bus would be traveling a completely different route and would not be taking me where I wanted to go.

As I rode along, the bus began to get more crowded at each stop, with more and more people getting on as I got closer to the transfer point, until after the 7th or 8th stop, there were so many people on the bus, and so many people standing between the seats, that you could not see out the windows. I kept repeating the number of the last stop to myself until I reached the next one. Then I would go up by one number and keep repeating that number until I got to the next stop, etc.

I finally got to the 17th stop and got off, just like Lollipop told me to. However, there was no sign of Lollipop any place I could see. I checked my watch and it wasn't quite 7:00 yet, so I assumed she would appear in a few minutes.

I started getting a little nervous when she still hadn't shown up by 7:15, was getting very nervous when she still hadn't arrived at 7:20 and started pacing back and forth and talking to myself when she still wasn't there at 7:25.

Finally, a taxi pulled up to the curb and Lollipop got out at just after 7:30. She immediately ran up to me and said "Michael, I am so sorry! My alarm did not go off! What time did you get here?"

"A little before 7:00", I answered.

A look of pure horror came over her face.

"Oh, no! Oh, Michael, I am so sorry! I have failed you on the very first day of your classes! I am so ashamed!"

"Okay, okay, don't worry! We'll work it out!" I told her. "Where do we go to get on the next bus?"

"Oh, we cannot take a bus now. It will take too long. We must take a taxi!" she answered.

I knew the language school would reimburse me for bus and subway fares, but I wasn't sure about taxis.

"Who's going to pay for that?" I asked.

"I will pay!" she answered.

"Well, I can pay half of it."

"No, I must pay. It is my duty!"

Well, I wasn't going to argue with her since I had to endure the waiting period, not knowing where she was or how to contact her. So she flagged down a taxi, told the driver where we had to go and off we went.

We actually just made it to the school on time, and there I learned that part of my duty as a foreign teacher was to stand in front of the main entrance with Lollipop and greet each kid who came walking into the school. The fact that the school had a foreign English teacher was considered a mark of very high status, and the principal wanted to make sure the parents and grandparents who brought the kids to school saw me.

Once the greeting part of my job was done, I was ready to begin my first class. However, the school also served breakfast to the kids, so if they didn't finish their breakfast on time, I had to wait. The teachers' assistants dished out the breakfast to the kids and they told me I could have a bowl of whatever they were eating too, but I didn't particularly like the looks of what looked like gruel anyway, so I always passed. Besides, I didn't want to run the risk of having to use the toilets at the school.

You have to understand something about the toilets in China. They aren't like the kind that most Americans and Europeans are used to. We had a "western style" toilet in our apartment, which meant it was one you could sit on, but for most places in China, the toilet was a ceramic covered hole in the floor with two footprints or tiles on either side, which is where you were supposed to put your feet, while you squatted to do your business. It had a foot pedal on one side which was what you stepped on to flush it once you were finished, but it was not a position which came naturally to me, and it took a little bit of practice before I was able to use one of these toilets with any confidence.

Needless to say, I tried not to use them unless it was absolutely necessary because of what I considered to be a design flaw, even though the Chinese didn't seem to have any problem with it. Plus, whenever you went to a public bathroom, you had to make sure to bring your own toilet paper. This was a luxury the Chinese did not normally have in public toilets. On top of that, the school toilet for teachers and visitors doubled as a janitor's closet, so included with the floor toilet and a sink, there were various mops, brooms and buckets stacked up, and you had to be careful when you squatted not to knock anything over. When you were done, you had to make sure you had enough toilet paper to finish the job, and you could wash your hands in the sink, but there wasn't any towel or cloth to use to dry them. For all of these reasons, I tried to make going to the bathroom at the schools a rare event.

I had a schedule that required me to teach 5 classes of 30 minutes each at the morning school before leaving for 3 classes at the afternoon school. So I taught exactly 2 and a half hours at the morning school, followed by an hour and a half of classes at the afternoon school for a grand total of teaching classes for 4 hours per day, three times per week. A ridiculously easy job, right?

Well, not exactly. The bus trip on two buses to get to the morning school took 2 hours. These weren't 2 comfortable hours by any stretch of the imagination, either. If I was lucky, there was sometimes a seat on the first bus, but more often than not, I would have to stand in a bus packed like a sardine can. As more and more people got on at each stop, the bus got more and more crowded, until I was literally wedged between at least 4 or 5 other passengers for the entire trip. I could sometimes get a glimpse of the outside world passing by through a small unblocked section of a window, but mostly I counted the stops and learned where I had to get off to catch the second bus.

The second bus was even worse. Since I was now getting on a bus which had already been traveling along most of its route, it was already jam packed by the time I got on, this time with Lollipop, who would meet me at the transfer point. Now I had to try to squeeze my way into the bus between another 6 or 7 bodies and travel about another hour without being able to see anything except the backs of the people in front of me. Because of an injury to my back a couple of decades earlier, I cannot stand for very long in one place without getting a sharp ache in my lower back. In addition, if I have to stand for much longer than 30 minutes or so, I can get random shooting pains in my legs. During a normal day for me in America, this hardly ever happened, but with a two hour commute, crushed between a busload of other people, it happened every trip. And the longer it took, the worse it got, so I was not thrilled with having to take this trip each morning when I taught classes.

Once we arrived at the school and finished our greeting duties for the first 20 minutes, we had to wait another 10 or 15 minutes for the kids to finish their breakfast. Then I was finally ready to start teaching.

I had to bring everything I was going to use for my classes inside a backpack, which included folders with pictures, CDs with musical lessons and posters, which had to be rolled up and stuck outside the backpack. Then, once I was there, Lollipop and I had to go into a classroom, say hi to all the kids, try to get them to settle down and then teach them some vocabulary, along with a few word games with pictures and/or drawings, and one of the musical CDs. I had to cue the Chinese teacher in the room to play the CD at the right time, and since they tended to treat my half hour in the classroom as an unofficial break, they didn't always pay attention to what I was doing and I would have to call out the "cues" loudly 3 or 4 times.

We would try to squeeze in some vocabulary lessons, a musical CD and a couple of games to get the kids involved and entertained. All of the classes were monitored by a closed-circuit camera, so the parents could always go online to see what was happening in the kids' classrooms. So it was important to keep the kids entertained, as well as trying to educate them, or the parents could call the school and complain that they expected more for their tuition payments.

Once the games were done, I had a supply of stickers to give to the kids who came up with the right answers. This was like having the keys to the candy store because the kids treasured these things like they were made out of gold! I started with simple stars that I would stick on the kid's arm or shoulder whichever they preferred – some even wanted to have it stuck to their foreheads - but soon found out that if I could use stickers of cartoon characters, the kids would try even harder. For some reason, getting a sticker with a Flintstones or Disney character on it was the kind of prestige money couldn't buy for the kids in my classes!

At the end of our 30-minute class (which felt more like a performance) we would tell the kids it was time to leave and wave goodbye. Since these were 4 and 5 year old children we were dealing with they were still very sweet and affectionate. Most of them would run up to me and Lollipop and wrap their arms around our legs, begging us not to go. We definitely got a feeling of appreciation from them, but we had to rush out to get to the next class.

The next class might be on the same floor, or it could be on the second or third floor of the building. I had to draw up a cheat sheet to use on any days Lollipop wasn't there to remember where I had to go for each class. There was no time allowed to get from one class to another either, so Lollipop and I would rush through the hallway with my backpack full of cards, pictures, CDs and posters to get to the next classroom because each class was supposed to get a full 30 minutes of instruction. Obviously, since it took 3 or 4 minutes to get from one class to another, this was impossible to do, but we tried to keep the time it took to transfer between classes to a minimum to avoid parental complaints.

When our classes were finished at approximately 11:00 a.m., Lollipop and I would walk to the lunchroom in another building behind the school. We had about 45 minutes for lunch, which was provided by a kitchen staff for me and Lollipop and the teachers and students from another mid-level school directly behind the grammar school where we taught. There were probably around a hundred students from the middle school, along with about a dozen teachers eating in this lunchroom beside us, so it took a while to get through the line to the servers' counter. You also had to bring your own Tupperware or plastic bowl, and/or eating utensils, because the school provided only the food.

The good news was the lunch was completely free. The bad news was you had to eat it.

It didn't change very often. It was always some form of unrecognizable stew or vegetables with a mixture of pureed something or other, and occasionally a piece of chicken or pork. It really wasn't all that bad, but the fact that I hadn't eaten for about 7 hours may have had something to do with that. Plus, for some strange reason, there was never anything to drink, not even water. Apparently, this was a luxury the school did not feel compelled to provide.

After lunch, Lollipop and I would start our journey to the afternoon school. The first day there, Lollipop told me "We must go to the bus stop for the bus for the afternoon school. But first we must take a tricycle."

"A tricycle?" I asked.

"Yes, a tricycle!"

I thought she must have meant something else, but then I saw what it was. It was actually a three wheeled motorized bicycle, with a home-made carriage, or passenger compartment mounted on a frame built over the bicycle to create a miniature 3 wheeled taxi. We would hail one of the tricycle drivers who rode up and down on the street outside the school, and pay the driver to take us to the bus stop for the afternoon school.

Lollipop taught me how to tell the driver where I wanted to go in Chinese, for those rare occasions when she couldn't join me. I don't know how you spell it or write it, but it sounded something like "Yow, jee-oh leeal, chone tee!" However, every time I said it for practice, the driver would just stare at me and look confused. Then Lollipop would say it and he would nod and start to drive.

Once we finished with our 15 minute ride by tricycle, we would stand by the side of the road to catch the afternoon bus. This was in an area where there was a huge amount of construction going on, which meant the road was always either muddy or dusty. When it was muddy, you could step around the mud most of the time, but when it was dry it was very dusty. Depending on how windy it was you might have to stand in a mini-dust storm until the afternoon bus arrived because there was no shelter of any type available. On one or two occasions, the dust was so bad it made both Lollipop and I cough. I tried not to say anything, since I knew it wasn't going to change anyway, but after one very bad coughing fit, Lollipop had to yell "I HATE THIS PLACE!"

I felt like telling her I understood why.

Then, once the afternoon bus finally arrived, we had another hour's ride, again standing nose to nose with a load of other sardines, I mean people, sandwiched into the bus. Occasionally, we did get a seat, but because this route went through more sections of the city that were under construction, the potholes we hit on the unpaved roads could literally knock you out of your seat. Plus, if you were sitting anywhere near the back, at times the rear exit door would not close completely, so we would find ourselves in the middle of a cloud of dirt and dust which would blow through the door every time the bus started or stopped.

After our *pleasant* ride to the afternoon school, we got to sit for about an hour and 15 minutes while the kids at that school had their afternoon nap after lunch. Then I was able to teach 3 classes of thirty minutes each, one right after another, boom, boom, boom – just like at the morning school. Only these students were a little older – 5 and 6 year olds- and a lot rowdier. Any time I tried to use the musical CDs or let the class play a vocabulary related game it turned into chaos because the kids were already wound up and itching to get done and go home.

On a few of these occasions, I tried to wave to the Chinese teacher sitting at the back of the room, who was supposed to be there to help control the kids in situations like these, but instead, she was usually checking her email or listening to her iPod and not paying much attention to anything I might be doing. At one point I got so frustrated, trying to make the kids quiet down, I picked up the end of one of the long tables they sat at, instead of desks, and banged it on the floor 4 or 5 times very loudly. When the kids finally stopped chattering and looked at me I "yelled" (although for me, it was a pretty quiet yell) "Quiet down!', followed by the obligatory finger in front of the lips along with a "Shhhhhhh"-ing sound.

This seemed to finally get their attention and I could proceed. The next day, however, Lollipop told me that some of the parents had seen this event on the closed-circuit TV feed to the internet, and had called the school to complain that I was yelling at the kids.

"You cannot bang the table on the floor, Michael. The parents do not like it."

After that I had to use hand claps and whistles, but the only thing that ever worked was yelling louder than the kids' chattering. When I was in school, I never understood why the teachers always got so mad about the students talking in class. Now I understood.

Once the afternoon classes were done, it was time for Lollipop and I to wait outside in the courtyard in front of the school to do our "afternoon goodbyes", similar to the "morning hellos" we did at the morning school. The only difference here was that some of the kids wanted to introduce me to their parents or grandparents who were picking them up to go home.

Since the students at this school were a year or two older than the kids at my morning school, I would start each class by having them all stand up and stretch their arms up, then out, then down. Then I would stand up and shake my body and head at the same time and make a sound created by shaking my head and lips while vocalizing a slurping noise. I don't really have a name for it, but I guess you could call it the "bbbllawwwwwwwwwww" sound.

The kids would mimic what I was doing. I would do it 3 or 4 times and they absolutely loved this. They had been sitting in the classroom all day long, with no real recreational periods except for meals since the time they started, and they most likely would have to continue with some type of training or tutoring as soon as they got home, so this was a great way for them to blow off steam for a few minutes. They loved doing it so much that when Lollipop and I were standing in the courtyard when they were getting picked up to go home, some of them would come up to me with their parent or grandparents in tow and say "Michael! Michael!" Then they would shake their heads and bodies and make the "bbbllawwwwwwwwwwww" sound to their parents' or grandparents' delight.

After we finished all our goodbyes to the kids, Lollipop and I would part company, and I would get on the bus to return to my apartment. This would be another bus ride of about an hour and a half, again in a bus with wall-to-wall people, and again I almost always had to stand for the entire trip, feeling the ache in my back and legs once more.

I still had about a 6 block walk once I got off the bus, so I generally got back to my apartment a little after 6:00 pm. Although I only taught classes, and got paid for teaching for a total of 4 hours, my entire work day including travel to, from and between the schools combined with the waiting periods for naptime, etc. totaled up to well over 12 hours! In addition, neither Yolande nor I received any support from the school agency, so we often had to make our own vocabulary cards, puzzles and game pieces for our classes during the two days per week I was supposed to be "off". Needless to say, this was beyond inefficient. If it wasn't for the actual class time that I spent with the kids, it would have been absolutely intolerable.

The commute was one of many things we were not told about before we made our commitment.

After putting up with the grueling commute to and from the schools I taught at 3 times per week for a little more than a month, I decided to tell Ernie it was time to find a teacher who could teach kindergarten classes, and find accommodations closer to the schools for him or her so that I could be reassigned to teach the IELTS classes that I had supposedly been hired for. I told him how having to stand through the morning and afternoon commute was causing shooting pains in my legs and I couldn't take it much longer. This wasn't entirely true, but it wasn't entirely false either. The pains in my legs were actually getting more intense and more frequent with each day. Although it was still far from the level where I couldn't actually stand it, I didn't think it was fair to make me wait until it was. So I told him I could only teach the kindergarten classes for about two more weeks. He told me to please continue until he could find a replacement and promised me he would have one within the next two weeks.

After two weeks had rolled around and there was still no indication that a replacement had been found, I called him again to ask him what the status was. He advised that he would be in Shenyang the next week and he would like to meet Yo and I for dinner. We could meet him at the language school office after Yo's classes on one of the days I didn't have classes.

I met Yolande at her afternoon school after she had finished teaching for the day on a Thursday afternoon and we took a bus to meet Ernie at the meeting place he had selected near the office. He was still as friendly and outgoing as ever, and he suggested a restaurant we could walk to that specialized in "western" style food. Since these types of restaurants were relatively few and far between in Shenyang, we gladly agreed.

Since Ernie was fluent in Mandarin, he took over ordering our food at the restaurant, which was a lot easier than trying to communicate with the waiter or waitress with sign language. After he had placed our order, I felt like it was time to get down to brass tacks.

"So how much longer is it going to be until I can start teaching the IELTS class?" I asked.

Ernie took a deep breath and looked away from me. "I don't know" he said.

I don't know? *I don't know?* You got me to come halfway around the world to teach college age students and business people who wanted to relocate to an English-speaking country for school or business, and now you tell me *you don't know* when I'll be able to start? *Why did you have me come here in the first place?*

I was about to ask him all these questions when he continued.

"The school hasn't been able to enroll enough students to make teaching a class worthwhile. You will still teach it once we have enough students, but I don't know when that will be."

"Well, I can't keep teaching the kindergarten classes much longer", I told him.

"I know", he said before I could finish. "We will have a new teacher in place within the next two weeks."

"That's what you said two weeks ago!" I said, trying to keep my temper under control.

"Yes, I know, and I take full responsibility for that. I have been trying to find qualified teachers to come, but it's difficult to do it now that the school year started two months ago. Most people looking for teaching jobs in China have already been hired", he explained.

I was ready to pull out my contract and show him what we had agreed to, but he stopped me by saying, "The good news is, I think I found someone."

At last, some good news!

"But he won't be able to start for another two weeks."

"Right!" I answered. "And what happens if he changes his mind and doesn't show up in two weeks?"

"If we don't have a new teacher to take over your classes in two weeks, I will teach the classes myself."

I thought about this for a few minutes, and I was starting to wonder if I should believe Ernie, but he seemed like such a genuinely likeable guy, I felt like I had to give him the benefit of the doubt.

"Okay," I told him. "Two weeks."

At the end of the two-week period, Ernie was still waiting for his new teacher to arrive - an Englishman named Tom – so he talked me into teaching for one more week. I told him I would do it, but this was definitely the last week for me to teach the kindergarten classes.

Before I could quit, however, I had one more detail to take care of.

The language school agency had never observed me teaching any of my classes, and for some reason they felt like they had to do it during my last week of teaching. Not only did they decide they would come to evaluate me during the last week of my classes, they actually scheduled the observation for the next to the last *day* of my classes. It didn't really make much sense, but if that's what they wanted to do, I didn't really care. I would be done after that Friday, one way or another.

So, at the start of one of my afternoon classes, on the next to last day of teaching the kindergarteners, Madame Zhou, Sky and Smile walked into the classroom and sat at 3 empty desks in the last row.

I had decided from the first week that simply repeating words and having the class recite them back to me wasn't really teaching anything. The kids that knew the words would answer when the whole class repeated the vocabulary words and the ones that didn't just sat there. The only way to get all the kids involved was to find a way to get them to talk and participate on one-to-one exercises.

The only problem with that was, since the classes I was teaching were only 30 minutes long, it didn't allow enough time to teach 20 kids much on a one-to-one basis. So I made up games in which the kids had to participate in to have the right to answer a question or point out a picture that represented the words or colors or numbers I was teaching them. I would cut up straws so I could have a handful of long and short straws in my hands and ask the kids to pull one out. If it was a short straw, they could go to the board and try to answer a question or write the name of a color or picture, etc. The kids were usually pretty excited about this because going up to the board and giving the right answer meant they would probably get a sticker, which, as I mentioned before, was the highest status symbol they could attain in their world. So, even though not every kid got to participate, it did keep all of them interested, and made learning a little more fun from their point of view.

However, I knew the triumvirate of Madame Zhou, Sky and Smile would not be pleased when they saw me trying to do some one-on-one teaching instead of just continuing with the repetitive group recitations. But, since it was my next to last class, I didn't really care. However, I did hope that they might see how excited and interested the kids seemed to be using this approach and see the value in using something more creative than rote repetition.

Unfortunately, I could tell by the silence from the "gang of three" at the end of my class that they were not impressed, and the phone call I got from Ernie Chang later that evening confirmed it.

"Michael, you shouldn't try to do one-on-one teaching. You don't have enough time."

"Well, it doesn't do any good for the kids who don't get it by using the group approach. The only way to get through to them is to get them to answer questions on their own, and they never do that if you just use the group recitation approach."

"Well, that's the way we've always done it and we don't want to have it changed now", Ernie answered.

At that point, I reminded him that I would only be teaching one more day before Tom took over anyway, and he agreed that it didn't really matter much what I did at that point. I told him I would complete the last day of teaching kindergarten classes as we agreed and that Tom would have to take over the following week. He agreed that that was what would happen, and then I asked him again how long I would have to wait until the IELTS classes could begin. He said he didn't know, but would check in with me on a weekly basis to let me know what progress had been made.

He kept his promise for the first two weeks, but didn't call after that unless I called him first. As it turned out, I waited a solid month, surfing the net in my apartment all day and watching what few programs there were in English on television, waiting to be notified that the IELTS classes were ready to begin.

By the end of November I had taught classes for just under two months and had been sitting around in my apartment waiting to teach the IELTS classes for nearly as long, and I was just about fed up with teaching English in China.

****

Meanwhile, Yo was having similar problems in the schools she was teaching in. The language school agency had observed one of Yolande's classes, and even though the kids in her classes seemed to test out extremely high on vocabulary quizzes, she was also told that she should not divide her students into groups and that she should stick to teaching the entire class by rote and repetition. She was even more annoyed than me about this, and, unlike me, she was still teaching classes. I was sitting around in our apartment all day waiting for Ernie to call to let me know when I could start teaching the IELTS classes. But the straw that broke the camel's back was the working visa problem.

We had entered China on tourist visas, which were only valid for 90 days, with the understanding that the agency that hired us would be able to process the paperwork required to allow us to obtain a permanent work visa before the tourist visas expired. As it got closer and closer to the deadline, we sent emails to Ernie, Sky and Madame Zhou several times asking for the status. Each time we received an answer that the documents had been submitted and we would receive our permanent work visas well before the expiration date.

When it got down to three days before the expiration date, I called Ernie to find out what the status was again.

"We are having a problem getting the government to release the visas," he said.

What kind of a problem, I asked

"Nothing big, just the usual problem with the bureaucracy in China," he said.

But what if we don't get the visas before our current visas expire?

"Don't worry. It will not be a problem. They have actually approved the permanent visas but they have not released them yet."

But we did worry. After all, we had seen and heard about U.S. citizens and other people working temporarily in China or North Korea who had been held as prisoners for being caught without a valid visa and treated like they were spies. A lot of these stories were probably exaggerations and some of them may have been more complicated than our situation, but we didn't really want to wait to find out if it would cause us any type of problem regarding our freedom to come and go when we wanted to. When it got down to two days before the deadline, Yolande and I made a big decision. She was going to call in sick for the next two days and we were going to terminate our contract with the language school agency if the visas did not come through in time.

The day that Yolande called in sick, Madame Zhou and the agency got very suspicious. They knew that Yo was unhappy about the interference and negative critiques she had been getting regarding her teaching methods, and they suspected she wasn't really sick in a physical sense, but staying home from class as a protest. There really wasn't anything they could do about it, but the problem we had was that, since neither of us would be in the classroom before we gave notice of our termination in two days, we would have to go to the agency office in person the next week to collect the pay we had coming. Of course, if the permanent visas actually did come through before the termination notice, it would be more difficult to explain why we were quitting.

The real reason was that we were both tired of putting up with the interference from the agency, the school principals and in my case, the lies involved regarding the IELTS classes, which resulted in my total inactivity for over a month. We had essentially lost all trust in the agency, and decided that, even if the visas did come through in time, we had enough reasons to quit anyway. We believed the agency had breached their contract with us by not having the IELTS classes that I was hired for, and also by not providing the free Chinese lessons we were supposed to receive. I did attend 3 meetings with Sky and Smile at the agency's office before the week of our showdown, in which they attempted to teach me some Chinese phrases, but these were hardly what I considered lessons. There was no structure, curriculum or study materials involved, so it was obvious they were simply trying to substitute the meetings for actual, planned lessons. Besides, they were supposed to provide the lessons for both of us, not just me.

The biggest questions were, what would they try to do to keep us from quitting and would we have any hope of getting the wages due to us for the lessons we had already taught, or would they ignore our charges or have them invalidated in their judicial system? After all, we didn't know anything about how business law was conducted in China, and for all we knew it would simply be treated as their word against ours, and we did not think we would have an advantage in a situation like that. Even more important, would they take any actions to try to keep us from leaving? Since we were the outsiders, we didn't know what kind of legal problems might await us if we tried to quit, whether or not we had valid grounds.

But the bottom line was that we couldn't stand the thought of being trapped there in the situation we had to deal with for another 9 months, as our original contract required. So we decided we would go ahead and submit our termination notices the day after our temporary visas expired, whether the permanent visas came through or not.

The day before our temporary visas were to expire, I sent a final email to the language school agency who had been assuring us for the last 3 weeks that the permanent visas would be issued in time. I sent a message to the language school rep and also copied Ernie Chang and told them in no uncertain terms that if we did not get our visas by the next day we would be terminating our contract and would not teach any more classes. The big day came and went and, just as we suspected, we received emails from the agency advising us that, due to unforeseen circumstances, the permanent visas had not been issued yet, but they were working with the government agency involved to get this problem resolved as soon as possible. Not to worry! "You will be paid for all your classes and may continue to teach until the permanent visas are received", the email said (or words to that effect).

That was the email we were waiting for. If the agency hadn't been in violation of our contract before, they definitely were now. We knew that, based on a strict interpretation of the law, we could not legally work in China without a valid working visa, and since we still did not have one, this definitely gave us grounds to terminate the contract. I sent an email to all of the agency personnel that we had email addresses for, including Ernie Chang, to advise him that we were terminating our contract and would be leaving Shenyang the following weekend (Yolande had the foresight to make reservations for a two week "farewell tour" of China so that we could see the sights we had always hoped to see before we left.)

As I expected, within an hour of sending the email message, my phone rang and I could see that the caller was Ernie Chang. I decided not to answer the call. It would not change anything and I didn't have the heart to argue with him. I knew that he was caught in the middle, and I still genuinely liked him, but we weren't going to change our minds about leaving, so I didn't see the point.

Ernie left a voice mail message assuring us that everything was taken care of and that somehow the agency had secured a legal work permit for us, even though the permanent visas had not yet been issued. I didn't know how they could have done that, and in reality, I didn't care. They had used up all their excuses and it was time to cut the cord.

Of course, it wasn't without some pain on our part. We had to give up almost 4 months of our prepaid lease and a security deposit, and would not be reimbursed by the school for our flight out of China, which was part of our agreement if we had completed the contract according to its original terms. But that seemed like a small price to pay to get out of Shenyang and find a decent job somewhere else in the world.

We got several more phone calls from Ernie as well as emails. One of his emails mentioned that he could not fix things for us "if you will not pick up the phone". I knew he was right, but by this time, we really didn't want anyone to fix anything. We had had enough of the lip service and half-truths we had to put up with, along with the interference related to our teaching methods, so we were more than ready to go. After 3 or 4 days, when Yolande did not show up for her classes at either school, (which is what we had told them would happen), Ernie finally gave up and let us know that we could collect our final wages that week at the agency's office.

The agency had already hired another teacher to take my place and they had a new one arriving within a few days to take Yolande's place. Either Ernie or Ms. Zhou had to teach Yolande's classes in the meantime. I felt a little bit bad about this, but then Yolande reminded me about the lack of support and lies and/or lip service that we had had to put up with, and she reminded me that they didn't respond to any of our complaints, so there was no reason to feel sorry for them. Sorry or not, we couldn't back down now and about 4 days after we had sent our termination notice, it was time to go to the agency office to collect our final wages.

I was a little surprised that they didn't withhold our wages in an attempt to force us to stay, but I had already warned them that if they tried to do this, I would make sure to let all potential foreign teachers know what they were getting themselves into with this agency via viral internet postings on the TEFL and EFL teachers' websites, and I guess they felt it wasn't worth the risk.

We arrived at the agency's office building and took the elevator up to the 4th floor, where they were located, not knowing exactly what to expect. We had to walk into the main office and face Ms. Zhou, who seemed to take a dislike to us from the very beginning and wasn't about to get friendly now. However, as soon as walked through the doorway, she turned and said something in Chinese to Sky, who was also there, and she greeted us and led us into a separate room.

Sky was not very happy about the whole situation and she let it show. She was already not too happy with me because I had disagreed with the way she had allocated my wages during a prior payment. I can't remember how it came about, eventually Ernie told her to pay me the amount I claimed was due and of course, she resented being overruled. In spite of this, she made sure she paid us the exact amounts due for all the classes we had taught up until the date of our termination notice. She definitely was not the warm and friendly assistant we had come to know a couple of months' earlier, but then, I'm not sure I would be warm and friendly either in her place.

I counted the wad of bills she handed me to make sure it was correct, which seemed to make her more hostile. I didn't do it to tick her off, though. I just wanted to make sure she hadn't miscalculated the amount due. When Yo and I were both satisfied that we had been paid correctly, we thanked her and she gave us a very stiff and formal goodbye, but then right before she left, she called in Smile and Lollipop and had us take pictures of all of them. Smile and Lollipop gave us both hugs and wished us well and vice versa. Lollipop even told me that the kindergarten kids kept asking her where I had gone. Again, I felt bad about leaving the kids behind, but knew it had to be done.

Having concluded our formal resignation by signing forms acknowledging that we had been paid all the wages due to us, etc., etc., we walked out of the office and felt the euphoria of having been released from our own private "jail". At the same time we felt sorry for Smile and Lollipop, who had expressed the same desire to us on a few occasions because we knew that under the current political situation, they would never be able to leave China and probably never be able to get a different job. That was one of the unfortunate facts of life in China and we would not be sorry to leave. But first, we had to see the sights we had waited for 3 months to experience. We weren't leaving China before we got to see the Great Wall!

****

Before we gave our notice to the agency, Yolande had made a very thorough itinerary as part of our plan to see the sights of China before we made our great escape. We started out with Beijing, where we saw Tiennamen Square, the Imperial Palace and some truly unique and creative sculptures in a part of the city known as "Section 798".

The main attraction, of course, was the Great Wall. We had to take a special bus to get there and when we did, we found that walking along the Great Wall in late November was like braving the wind and cold of Antarctica! When I say it was cold, I mean it had to be just about the coldest I had ever been, or at least it felt that way. In spite of this, there were still plenty of tourists walking along with us, taking pictures and apparently unaffected by the harsh, cold wind. It was an incredible sight, I admit, but after about 3 hours, we had to leave before we got frozen solid.

The next stop was Xian, where we saw the famous Terra Cotta Warriors. I wasn't that familiar with this attraction beforehand, but I soon learned some of the amazing history behind this excavation site. The excavation actually started by accident in a farmer's field back in 1974, and since that time, had unearthed literally hundreds and hundreds of terra cotta statues in the form of ancient medieval warriors. The reason for this was that an emperor from ancient times believed that he needed to take "warriors" with him when he died to protect him from the evil spirits in the afterlife. It was truly an amazing site, and well worth the trip to Xian.

After Xian, we headed on to Guillin, where we took a river cruise and again saw some incredible scenery, including a demonstration of birds trained to dive into the water to catch fish and bring them back to a fisherman on a raft. Once more, this was a "must see" trip which I was very fortunate to be able to experience.

Our last stop was Shanghai, which lived up to its reputation as China's most modern city. The skyline on the riverfront was very picture-worthy, especially at night, and we also enjoyed visiting the shops and restaurants in a popular tourist area called "Old Shanghai". Our "farewell tour" during our last two weeks in China almost made up for all the hassles and ineptitude we had experienced from the schools and language school agency during our classroom experiences. Still, all good things must come to an end, so after spending 3 days in Shanghai, it was time to return to Shenyang to make preparations for our final departure from China.

The whole trip went smoothly until we returned to Shenyang. When we got to the airport and went to the baggage carousel to collect our luggage, the temperature was so warm, I had to put down my laptop to take off my coat. The problem arose when I realized several minutes later that I didn't know where I left it. I searched all over the baggage area but could not find it anywhere. I gave my name, address, phone number and email address to a woman who spoke English at the lost and found booth and returned to our apartment, hoping that someone might find it and turn it in.

The next day, we went to the apartment of an English-speaking couple we had met during one of our explorations of Shenyang and asked if we could use their laptop to make a reservation for our flight back to Holland. Not only did they allow us to use their computer, our friend Lina, who was actually from Colombia, but spoke perfect English, even made lunch for us and her husband, Richard, who was a German engineer working at the local Mercedes plant.

We logged onto the computer and checked our emails and found out that, miraculously, someone had sent an email to us regarding my laptop! It turned out that a Shenyang cop, working at the airport had found it and sent an email asking me to send him a phone number he could reach me at. I did, he called, and the next day I took a taxi to the airport to meet him and retrieve my laptop.

He didn't speak much English, but thankfully, enough to tell me how to find his office at the airport. When I showed up, he insisted that someone take two pictures of him presenting the laptop to me. It seemed like returning an American's lost computer was a terrific photo opportunity which could be published in the local newspapers to show how Shenyang's police were helping foreigners like me. I felt it was a small price to pay to get my laptop back, so I gladly posed with him and shook his hand.

The next day we were packed and ready to take a plane to visit and stay with Yolande's parents in Holland until we figured out where our next adventure would take us. Our overall impression of China was it was a great place to visit, but you wouldn't want to work there – at least not as a foreign English teacher.

We had our apartment cleaned spic and span to prepare for an inspection by the landlord before we left. This time the landlady who had chewed me out on the first day we moved in was there, with her husband and her son. She was now in a much better mood than the first time we met. It probably had something to do with the fact that they were going to be keeping the four months of advance rent we had paid and would still be able to rent the apartment to someone else. She and her husband confirmed nothing had been damaged and were very happy with the cleanliness of the apartment, so they gave us a clean termination rating on the paperwork we had to complete before we left. After that we made a little small talk with her son, who was an advanced English student, but who was too shy to talk much to us. So we then said goodbye and carted our luggage down to the street to hail a taxi to take us to the airport.

It was now the first week of December and the part of China we lived in was in the far northeast, very close to North Korea. As most people know, the temperature can get very low in that part of the world in December, and as we stood on the street trying to flag down a cab we realized that we might have a problem.

Because most of the taxis in Shenyang were not designed to carry much luggage they generally had relatively small trunks and just enough space for about 4 passengers. Apparently, the amount of luggage we had stacked beside us on the sidewalk was more than most of the taxi drivers wanted to deal with. We had brought 2 large suitcases, 2 large backpacks and 2 carry-on bags in anticipation of being in China for a full year. We soon realized that getting a taxi to stop for us with that amount of luggage in view was going to be tricky.

Taxi after taxi drove by us, oblivious to our waves and yells as we stood there in the freezing cold. As the minutes dragged by, it became colder and colder. So cold, in fact, that we realized we might have to take desperate measures to get a taxi to stop for us and all our luggage.

Since we did not know how to call a cab company on our phone, we tried to call Lina and Richard, the friends we had met who allowed us to use their computer before I had retrieved mine at the airport. They didn't answer, but I left a message on their voice mail telling them our predicament, and asking them if they could somehow look up a local taxi company and call them to arrange our pick up for us. Maybe if they couldn't see all the luggage we had, they would send us a cab!

After waiting another ten or fifteen minutes, the cold was really, really getting to us. I didn't think we could take it too much longer, (or I should probably say, I didn't think *I* could take it too much longer), but we really didn't have any other options. We had turned in the keys to our apartment and we had too much luggage to drag with us inside a shop or restaurant nearby. Besides, if we did that we would just have to drag it all out again when and if we could finally get a cab to stop. I finally decided to call the only other person I thought could possibly help us – Sky!

I was pretty sure she wouldn't be exactly thrilled to hear from me. Not when the last time I saw her, she was obviously miffed that I counted the money she handed over to us for our final wages, and was definitely not happy that we were leaving long before our contract year was up. But desperate times call for desperate measures, so I took out my cell phone and dialed her number.

When she answered, she spoke in Chinese, saying something I obviously didn't understand, but I was pretty sure I recognized her voice.

"Sky", I said, "This is Michael, you know, from Michael and Yolande."

The long pause on the other end confirmed what I already knew, that I was the last person she wanted to talk to again.

"Yes, Michael, what is it, what is it, what is it you are calling, what is it you are calling me for?"

She always spoke English this way. I guessed that she had trouble remembering how to say the words she was trying to say in English toward the end of the sentence and repeated the first half two or three times until she could remember how to say the words at the end of the sentence.

"Sky, Yolande and I are trying to get a cab to get to the airport, but we can't get any to stop for us. I think they don't want to stop because they think we have too much luggage. Would you be able to call a taxi company and ask them to come get us so that we can get to the airport in time?"

I made sure I mentioned Yolande's name because I knew Sky was a lot fonder of her than she was of me, so the chances of getting her to do something to help Yolande were much higher than if I had asked her to do it for me alone.

Again, there was a long pause until she said "You want me, you want me, you want me to call a taxi for you?"

"Yes, because we can't get any to stop for us and it's really cold and we have to get to the airport to catch our plane."

This would have been the perfect time for her to get revenge on us, if that's what she wanted, by simply saying no. But to her credit, she continued to be professional.

"I will call, I will call, I will call a taxi for you. Please tell me, please tell me, please tell me where you are."

I gave her the location, which she knew from having visited us at our apartment a few times, and thanked her for her help. She said "You're welcome", but I could tell by her voice that she was not at all pleased at being asked to do a favor for someone she was not particularly fond of. At that moment, though I didn't really care, if she could find a way to get a taxi pick to us up and get us out of the fricking cold.

I told Yolande that Sky would call a taxi for her, but she was too cold to do anything but nod. We continued to try to flag down a cab and they continued to ignore us.

Finally, after an hour had gone by and it appeared that either Sky didn't call a cab after all, or they were just very slow in responding, Yolande told me "I'm going to go ask at the hotel if anyone can help us", referring to an international hotel just a short ways down the street,

"Okay", I told her, "but I don't think it'll do much good."

"Well, it can't hurt", she said.

I admired her ability to find ways to make the Chinese understand her, even though she didn't speak any more Chinese than me, but as she walked towards the hotel, I didn't think she would have any luck getting anyone to help us. Within 5 minutes, however, she emerged with a young Chinese man, dressed in a suit and tie and obviously one of the hotel staff, walking along behind her,

"He says he can get a cab", Yo said, and within another 5 minutes, he did exactly that. First he hailed the cab and when it stopped, he went over and talked personally to the driver. Whatever he said seemed to work, because the driver immediately got out, opened his trunk and helped us get our large suitcases in. Everything else had to go in the back seat with Yo or on my lap. The bottom line was, regardless of how we had to cram it in, we finally got out of the cold and on our way to the airport.

We thanked the man from the hotel profusely, but he seemed to simply want to get back inside the hotel. We certainly didn't blame him for that.

The last thing I had to do was call Sky back to let her know we already had a cab.

"Hello, Sky, this is Michael again. Um…did you call a cab to pick us up?"

"Yes, I called, I called, I called for a taxi a few minutes ago."

"Yeah, well, you can call them and cancel it. We just finally got a cab."

Another long pause.

"You have, you have a taxi now?"

"Yes, we just finally got one to stop. So you can call and cancel the other one."

"Alright, I will, I will, I will call", she said. Then she hung up. I think she was just as glad to be rid of us, as I was to be rid of her. But I have to give her credit – regardless of her personal feelings, she tried to be a true professional and help us. No matter how we felt about everything else, I definitely respected her for that.

Interlude

*"You can't always get what you want
But if you try sometime, you just might find
You get what you need!"*

*-The Rolling Stones
You Can't Always Get What you Want*

It's 4:00 a.m. and I wake up to realize I'm lying on a mattress on the floor next to the mattress my wife is lying on in my in-laws' house in Holland. The next thing I realize is the reason I'm awake, which is because I have to go the bathroom. This presents at least two problems: one, I have to crawl off the mattress without accidentally pushing down on my wife's mattress and waking her up, and two, I have to put on some pants to cover myself from the time I open the bedroom door until I get into the bathroom.

I have to put on some pants because I'm still not ready to let my mother-in-law see me walking around in my underwear. She is 80 years old, and because she is suffering from ALS, she is awake for most of the night, and her bedroom lies directly across from the bedroom where we are sleeping in our makeshift bedroom. In addition, she always keeps her door open, so if she is awake, and she often is, she will see me emerge from the bedroom on my way to the bath room in my skivvies. I know that's not exactly a serious problem, but I'm still insecure enough to try to limit such presentations to my wife and doctor. In addition, it probably wouldn't offend her or upset her at all, but it's still something I'm not comfortable with, so I struggle to put on my pants in the dark, bracing my butt against the wall to keep from falling onto my wife.

After I manage to get my pants on, I bravely march out into the hallway, trying to be as silent as possible, and hope that she is asleep and won't see me. Unfortunately, as I open the door, I can see she is lying in bed with the light on and Kwartel the cat appears to be sitting on the bed with her. I quickly plod down the hallway to get to the bathroom in time and answer the urgent call from Mother Nature. Once I finish, however, I still have to walk back through the gauntlet and hope I can open the door and disappear into the bedroom without being noticed. Unfortunately, Lady Luck is not with me tonight, for before I can get through the door, I hear her call me.

"Mike", she cries out in a plaintive tone, "De poes!"

I have no choice but to face the music, so I walk into her room to try to determine exactly what she wants. Fortunately, this time it seems pretty clear that she simply wants the cat removed. Pointing to the cat I ask, "You want me to take her?" "Yah!" is the simple reply.

I consider myself lucky since there have been times when she tries to communicate to me in Dutch what she wants me to do, and because my fluency in Dutch is so poor, it may take a few minutes and several questions for me to comprehend what she needs. This time, it is fairly straightforward: get the cat out of here!

Now the question of what to do with her comes up, because Kwartel is a persistent old feline. If I put her in the living room and just close the door she will meow at the top of her lungs until she gets what she wants. My guess is that, since she has a thyroid problem that keeps her underweight no matter how much she eats, that she is probably hungry again. So I take her into the kitchen and dish out a quarter can of cat food for her. Sure enough, she eats it up like it's her last meal.

Now that I've been able to achieve my goal of getting to the bathroom in time, and feeding the cat to boot, I walk quietly back to the bedroom. I assume my mother-in-law's needs have been fulfilled, but I try to get into the bedroom quickly, just in case.

As I open the door, I hear her call out in a quiet, thankful tone, "Thank you".

Suddenly I feel ashamed for being so selfish about trying to avoid a long interruption in my sleep. How petty that now seems, compared to someone who needs help getting into bed, turning over and being able to go to the bathroom herself. Even though she has caregivers who come into the house twice during the night to help her perform these tasks, there are times when she still needs someone else for minor problems that come up on a random basis.

It's a sad situation, and one that can be quite irritating at times, especially to my wife and father-in-law, who must bear the brunt of her daily care. She is often uncooperative and unreasonable, afraid to try to do things for herself and depending on others more than necessary. Still, I wonder how pleasant I would be in her situation and pray that I never find out.

As I crawl back onto my mattress in the dark, I can't help but wonder why some people are forced to endure illnesses like this and how some people, like me, have had a relatively problem free life, from a health and medical viewpoint. I guess you shouldn't really question these things, so I close my eyes and try to go back to sleep. Before I drift off, I make sure to thank the Higher Power that the biggest problem I have is whether or not somebody will see me in the hallway in my underwear. At least that's how it seems.

Chile

"Each time I find myself lyin'
Flat on my face
I just pick myself up and get back in the race"

-Dean Kay and Kelly Gordon
That's Life

After our 4-month adventure in China, we were extremely thankful to have someplace else in the world to return to and determine what we would do and where we would go next. We didn't know where we wanted to go, but we knew that our best bet to obtain a livable income while avoiding the corporate rat race would be to find another job as foreign English teachers. The dilemma was that I had a TEFL certificate, which, along with the fact that I was a native English speaker, allowed me to apply for a number of different foreign English teaching jobs, although I had no other education related credentials, while Yolande, who was perfectly fluent in English and had a master's degree in education to boot, but did not have a TEFL certificate, could not. It was a real Catch 22, and neither one of us knew if it was possible for both of us to find teaching jobs anywhere except for China. However, through the magic of the internet age, it only took about 3 days after we returned to Holland.

Don't get me wrong, being able to return to Holland and live with Yolande's parents rent-free for a temporary period was definitely a godsend for us after China. Unfortunately, Yo and her mother never had an extremely warm and fuzzy relationship, and having us around the house on a daily basis was not exactly something her mother enjoyed. She was never openly hostile, at least not to me, but she let it be known that she would be glad when we were gone so that things could get "back to normal", i.e. the way it was before we arrived. So it was again extremely fortunate that I discovered a website for foreign English teachers that advertised a job opening in Chile. In addition, it appeared that you did not need an advanced or more widely recognized TEFL certificate than the one which I had, and in fact, it seemed that they would also accept non-native English speakers!

I submitted our applications online and a few days later spoke to the hiring manager for the school via a Skype interview. Both Yolande and I talked to her and found out about the opportunity to come teach in Chile beginning in February. After a few preliminary documents were signed, scanned and emailed back, we had contracts to teach at a school in Antofagasta, Chile.

Neither one of us had ever heard of Antofagasta before, but it seemed like it would be more "foreigner friendly" than China. Monica, the hiring manager told us there were two movie cinemas, restaurants and a disco in town, and that we would be living rent-free in a high-rise apartment building with an oceanfront view. What's more, the daily commute to the school would involve a five minute walk. No busses, no subways, no trains – just a five minute walk! We couldn't wait to say yes fast enough!

We also made sure that we would not run into the same type of visa problems that we had in China. The hiring director had told us that the school would take care of all the details. On top of that, they would provide all the teaching materials, curriculum outline and two weeks of training to make sure we were ready and comfortable enough to handle the classroom. "Don't worry, Mike! We are not like China," Monica told me.

So, after another month in which Yolande's mother became increasingly impatient for us to leave, we boarded a plane that took us to Antofagasta, Chile, via stopovers in London, Madrid and Santiago. Although it might sound glamorous to have been in all these places, the reality was that all we ever saw of any of those cities was the inside of their airports. That really wasn't a concern, however, and we were happy to once again be leaving one country to go to another one half a world away.

The honeymoon lasted for roughly an hour after we landed in Antofagasta. The flights from Holland all went fine until we arrived at our final destination and found that one of our suitcases had been lost. This was not a big catastrophe, and it would eventually arrive a few days later, but it started things off on a less than pleasant foot. The bigger shock was waiting for us at our apartment.

Monica and the school principal picked us up at the airport and drove us to the apartment building where we would be living. The trip took about 45 minutes and as we drove along through the Atacama desert, we could see that we were not in a scenic wonderland, by any stretch of the imagination.

We had both seen deserts in the U.S. before, but nothing quite like the Atacama, which is actually the world's driest desert – so dry, that absolutely *nothing* grows there. Not cactus, not scrub grass, not tumbleweeds – nothing! The scenery passing by outside our car windows was strictly one of dry, barren mountains, surrounded by brown dirt and rocks, punctuated by small clusters of ramshackle buildings until we finally reached the city limits.

Although the structures in Antofagasta were not breath taking, they did appear to be relatively modern in contrast, and able to withstand the frequent earthquakes that that part of the world was known for. We drove by several industrial park areas and finally got into what Monica called "the nice part of town". It was definitely a step up from the areas we had just come through, but it still appeared to be what I would consider middle class homes in the U.S., surrounded by fences, walls or gates.

As we continued driving along the main road which paralleled the coast, we eventually came to the apartment building where we would stay. Monica had explained that three female teachers from Canada and a couple from the U.S. had already arrived the day before and had already had a problem.

It seemed that they had all gone to the disco in town the night before and nearly avoided a brawl caused by the fact that one of the Canadian teachers was a pretty blonde. Blonde hair on women is something of a rarity in Chile and it attracts males more rapidly than usual – especially in places where people drink alcohol, like a disco. Anyway, one of the male patrons in the disco decided he wanted to feel the blonde teacher's hair with his own hands, and one of the Chileans who was a boyfriend of a teacher at the school, and who was guiding the foreign teachers through the disco, came to the rescue. By all accounts, it was a very quick fight, and no one was seriously hurt. However, upon arriving back at the apartment, the Canadian teachers had broken the key to their room and had to call Monica at an ungodly hour in the morning to find a locksmith who could get their door open for them.

We all had a good laugh at this, except the school principal who was driving and did not seem particularly amused, but that could have been because he did not understand English very well. When we arrived at the apartment building we saw the three Canadian girls and the American couple sitting on a balcony on the second floor and waving hello to us.

They all seemed to be well recovered from their nocturnal adventure and quickly introduced themselves to us as we walked into our second floor apartment. We would be sharing our 3-bedroom flat with the American couple and the Canadian teachers would be living in the apartment next door.

The American couple's names were Kurt and Amy. Amy was a new teacher at the school, like us and the Canadian girls, but Kurt was simply Amy's boyfriend from Kansas City. Since the school provided apartments for teachers only, Amy and Kurt would only be staying in the same apartment as us for a few weeks. Everyone was pleasant and polite, but as we asked where our bedroom was so we could unpack our luggage, Kurt pointed to the last door in the interior hallway and said "Brace yourself".

As soon as we walked through the door, I understood what he meant. The bedroom had basically been trashed by whoever lived there before. The carpet was filthy, the bed had been left unmade, the sheets were dirty, there were food wrappers, potato chip bags, used Kleenexes, ants and even a condom or two lying all over the rug. It looked like it hadn't been cleaned in at least 6 months.

"We tried to clean most of it up when we got here yesterday, but we just ran out of time", Kurt said. We looked at him in amazement. "You mean it was worse that this?" I asked. "Oh, yeah!" he said. "Way worse!"

Yolande and I were astounded. This was the dirtiest bedroom we had ever seen, and now we would have to clean it up before we even thought about sleeping there. We asked Monica, who was still hovering around the front door after showing us in what happened.

"Yeah," she said, "The teachers who lived here last year had a big party before they left and made a huge mess."

That was definitely an understatement.

"When did they leave?" we asked.

"About a month ago."

"And nobody came in to clean it since then?"

"Oh, well the school cleaned it after they left when the classes were over in December and thought it was all cleaned and ready for the new teachers, but then the old teachers came back after it was cleaned and left it like this."

Somehow it didn't seem like we were getting the whole story, but since we were the newcomers, and there really wasn't much we could do about it, we decided to keep the complaints to ourselves and started to sweep mop and disinfect the room as much as we could. Amy and Kurt had thoughtfully washed some sheets and blankets for us the day before, so at least we could have clean bedding to sleep on. We spent the better part of the next three days cleaning the bedroom and also cleaning up the kitchen with Kurt and Amy's help, since that had also been left in a mess. Needless to say, this was not exactly the kind of place Monica had led us to believe we would be staying in during our Skype interview.

But that wasn't the last thing that would be different than the way it was described in that interview.

We arrived in Antofagasta a full two weeks before classes were scheduled to begin, ostensibly to provide two weeks of training for teachers who were new to the school, i.e. me, Yolande, Amy and the three Canadian girls. The first few days were basically orientation days intended to familiarize the new teachers with the school and the procedures to be followed for grading tests, homework assignments, etc. It also gave us a chance to meet some of the other teachers and get some feedback from them regarding the "real story" about working at the school.

Shortly after we had finally cleaned up the apartment to make it somewhat livable and had been introduced to how to get around town by bus to shop for groceries and anything else, we had an "open house" night where we basically left our door open for whoever wanted to join us. As some of the veteran teachers who had taught at the school last year began to filter in, we opened a few beers and turned on the radio, and pretty soon we had an apartment full of teachers from other floors in the building. It reminded me a lot of the impromptu parties we used to have back in my college days – which was actually very understandable, since most of the teachers were just a year or two out of college themselves, except for me and Yolande and a few others.

One of the first hints we got about what to expect from the school administration came when we were all sitting on our balcony, enjoying the warm summer night, having a few beers and generally comparing notes about living in the U.S., compared to Canada, England and Australia. Amy, who was probably the most excited of all of us to be there and extremely eager to start teaching, was talking to a few of the returning teachers and suddenly for some reason, she blurted out "Do you LOVE Monica?"

She was referring to our recruiter and director of the elementary grade teachers, and also my department head for two of the classes I was going to teach. I don't know what prompted her to ask it, but it was apparent by the long pause after her question, that "love" was not exactly the way some of the teachers felt about Monica.

"Sometimes" was the guarded reply, and I could tell by the way it was said that it really meant "not really". I wondered why the returning teachers would feel this way, but chalked it up to the fact that most people don't LOVE their bosses, no matter what kind of job they have, and this was probably no exception.

My doubts began to grow stronger, however after I spoke to Armando. Armando was a veteran teacher from Cuba, who had already taught at the school for 5 years. After joining me in a bottle of beer, he told me "There are four kinds of school administrations." He started to tick them off, one by one, lifting up a finger to emphasize each type of administration that he rattled off.

"One, you have an administration that's smart and works hard. Two, you have an administration that is smart, but doesn't work very hard. Three, you have an administration that is dumb, but works hard, and four, you have one that's dumb and doesn't work hard. We have the third kind – one that is dumb but tries to work hard."

Although it was somewhat comforting to hear that it wasn't the worst of the bunch, it was a little unsettling to think that the people who had hired us may have done it because they were too stupid to know any better. I asked him to explain why he said that but all he would tell me was "You'll see. You'll see."

Meanwhile the first week flew by with none of the training we had expected. We would walk to the school each day and spend 4 or 5 hours working on a long range lesson plan for each class we were teaching. Since I was teaching basic ESL English, English Literature and Medieval History, I had 3 separate lesson plans to prepare. I wasn't really sure how to go about this and surprisingly, there wasn't any instruction provided, just an edict that they had to be completed and turned into the department head before the Friday before classes began.

I reviewed the chapters of each subject I was supposed to teach and tried to guess how long each chapter would take to teach, what activities and homework I should try to include, etc., etc., etc. I thought once this was done, we would get into the training which Monica had assured us of during our Skype interview. However, once the lesson plans were completed, the next week was devoted to picking up the textbooks we would be using for each class, getting fitted for our school teacher's uniforms and revising the lesson plans we had created the week before. In short, Monica's comment to me during our interview about not worrying that we would have the same experience as we had in China turned out to be true. We wouldn't get just 3 hours of training before we started teaching real classes. We wouldn't get ANY training. So Monica was right. They definitely weren't like China in the training department. They were worse!

I kept hoping that Monica or someone else in the administration would get around to providing some last-minute training before we actually had to face the kids when the classes began, but no such luck. I finally realized on the Friday before the classes were scheduled to begin that the "training" we had been given was solely intended to instruct us on how to fill out class attendance sheets, grading standards and other administrative procedures. As far as how to deal with the kids was concerned, you were on your own.

I also remembered how Monica told me during our Skype interview that, even though I had no formal training as a teacher and had never taught elementary school subjects before, that I would be teaching the same class that she had taught the previous year and she would be able to help me every step of the way. When it came time to ask her to review my lesson plan for the entire year to see if I had allotted a reasonable amount of time to cover each particular chapter, however, she was always too busy trying to get her own lesson plans done. She was sure I had prepared a thorough schedule and that I would do a fine job with all my classes. So, when the first day of school finally rolled around, and I would have to face a classroom full of live 11, 12 and 13 year olds, I was terrified.

The first thing I realized when I entered the teachers' conference room around 7:30 that morning was how bloody hot it was! I happen to start sweating pretty easily when things get a little warm, and to me, it felt like I was walking into a sauna. None of the other teachers sitting at the conference table preparing their lessons seemed to mind, however so I assumed it was just something that only affected me for whatever reason. Unfortunately, I knew it wasn't my imagination from the copious amount of sweat rolling down the back of my neck. I felt even more self-conscious now, thinking that not only would the kids realize I didn't know what I was doing, but I would look like a drowned rat. If that didn't make me look stupid in the eyes of 6th and 8th graders, I didn't know what would.

My first class was scheduled to begin at 8:15. Unlike most of the other teachers, I had not been assigned to a home room, meaning I did not start the day by taking attendance and making school announcements first thing at 8:00 am. Since all the other teachers assembled in the conference room apparently were home room teachers, they all left to go to their classrooms shortly before 8:00 am, leaving me alone with my books and the schedule I planned on following the first day.

I assumed that another bell would ring at 8:15 when the students moved out of their home rooms to go to their first classes. However, when my watch indicated 8:15, there was no such sound. Nor was there any bell ringing at 8:16, 17 or 18. Nor would there be one at 8:20 or 8:25. I finally decided I had better go to my first classroom anyway, so I grabbed my books and my knapsack and headed bravely for the classroom.

When I got to my classroom, I found Armando, the Cuban teacher I had met during my first weekend in the apartment, sitting behind the desk.

"Are you teaching the first class here?" he asked as I walked in.

"Well, that's what they told me," I replied.

"OK, no problem," he said as he got up and walked out of the room.

"Don't go!" I wanted to say, but thought that might look just a little unprofessional. Instead, I sat down at the desk and faced my most horrible fear – the kids!

Actually, the kids in my first two classes weren't too bad. They were 8th graders, and with one or two exceptions, they were pretty respectful and cooperative. I really liked one of them. His name was Michael too, but I liked him because of his outgoingness and genuine interest in history (the subject I was teaching), and in the U.S. in general. We had a few conversations after class in which I tried to answer the multitude of questions he had regarding American society in general. This was the part of the job which was actually fun.

Unfortunately, I couldn't say the same for the rest of my classes. I was also teaching an ESL class for students who needed help learning basic English and grammar, and who were in the class because their English comprehension was unacceptably low. The biggest problem with this class was there were a couple of students in it who didn't speak English *at all!* Since my Spanish wasn't even good enough to be called *basic*, I couldn't even explain the lessons to him, and he couldn't understand any of the handouts

I issued or do any of the homework assignments, since they were all printed in English.

I didn't know what to tell him except "Sorry!" and ask him to sit and do the best he could – which he did - but I was amazed that the school would put a student who didn't speak any English in a class with a teacher who spoke almost no Spanish. However, I would soon learn that this wasn't the only instance in which this happened. In general, however, the kids in this class were still pretty cooperative and respectful.

Such was not the case with the 6th graders I had in two separate classes.

I had been told that all of the students in this school were extremely bright and creative, and they had been learning English since they were in pre-school, so there would never be a communications problem even if I spoke hardly any Spanish. Well, as I said, there were a number of things that we were never told, and two of them were: one, there were a few students in these classes that spoke no English as well, making any communication with them and any learning on their end to be impossible, and two, they may have been bright and creative, but there was really no way to tell since they were so fricking rebellious and uncontrollable!

I got my baptism under fire that first day with my first 6th grade classes in English Literature. I thought that by being friendly and easy going with the kids I would get them to like me and I would be able to break down any barriers between us, thereby making learning a fun activity for both of us.

I was totally unprepared for dealing with this breed of troublemakers, and they realized that pretty fast. I did my best to make the first day's class interesting and gave the kids a chance to tell me about themselves and I gave them a little bit of my background. I thought that would be a great way to break the ice and get them to enjoy learning. I didn't realize it at first, but all that really did was give them the impression that I was easy to manipulate and in the coming weeks they would find new and creative ways to annoy me and disrupt any attempts at serious teaching.

But that wouldn't happen for a few more weeks. In the meantime, I managed to find a way to have one of the most bizarre injuries of my entire life.

After the second day of classes, I was sitting on a chair in Monica's office along with three other teachers who, like me, were part of the English Literature department. Monica had called the meeting, because officially, as the department head, she needed to be updated on all of our classes' progress. The reality was that she and the other two female teachers wasted at least an hour of my time and the other male teacher's time by chatting about almost everything except that. Since I was the new kid on the block, I didn't feel it was my place to try to steer the discussion back to the classes, but Manuel, the other male in the group, decided at one point that he had heard enough and simply stood up and left. I wasn't brave enough to try a move like that yet, so I decided to stay put.

After another 30 minutes or so of inane drivel, Monica mercifully called the meeting to an end and allowed us to leave. As soon as I stood up from my chair, however, I knew something was wrong. I thought I heard a "snap" coming from my leg and I suddenly had a sharp pain behind my knee which caused me to limp severely.

I had already left Monica's office, so she and the other two teachers in Monica's office were still chatting away and didn't even notice anything had happened. However, with each step I took, the pain shot through me and I realized that I must have somehow pulled the hamstring in my left leg. I couldn't understand how I could have done that just by standing up from a sitting position in a chair, but it was just a freak accident that there really wasn't any explanation for.

I still limped to the school and taught all my classes for the next two days, but by doing so I made the injury gradually worse.

In addition, because I was teaching four different subjects, I had a lot more books to carry in my back pack than most, if not all the other teachers, and this put extra stress on my leg. On the morning of the third day after the initial injury, the pain was so bad I couldn't get out of bed.

I called the assistant principal at 6:00 am and told her I wouldn't be able to go to the school that day and didn't know how long I would be out. I had hoped it would only be one or two days, but as it turned out, I was laid up in the apartment and could barely walk any significant distance for almost two weeks.

The days seemed to drag on forever. There was only one book in English to read in the apartment, which was incredibly boring, and no matter what position I tried to assume I couldn't relieve the pain in my legs.

One of Yolande's co-workers gave us a ride into town one day after school so I could visit a doctor. Naturally, I had to have x-rays taken and I found out that I had managed to tear a hole in my hamstring muscle by trying to continue teaching after I initially pulled it. For a while, I was actually afraid that I might need surgery to fix it. However, the doctor gave me some pain pills and other medication, and after what seemed like an eternity of lying in bed all day for two full weeks, I was finally able to walk well enough to return to school.

While I was gone, the 6th graders grew cockier and were more than ready to resume their manipulation techniques by the time I returned.

I had never seen grammar school students behave the way they did at this school. My experiences as a 6th grader made me think that students at that age still felt it was necessary to listen to their teachers and stay in their seats unless they were given permission to leave. At Antofagasta, they seemed to think they had a right to get up from their desks and walk around the room whenever they felt like it. They also made a practice of rearranging their desks between classes to be able to sit next to their friends. On top of that, they felt they should be able to continue having private conversations even while the teacher was talking.

Naturally, I did not think these activities should be permitted in the classroom and I made sure I told them so as soon as I came back to the school. However, I soon found out that the school did not have any type of discipline policy and these kids knew it. No matter how many times I told them not to get up from their seats and walk over to their locker or the waste basket, or to stop talking while I was trying to explain, they paid little or no attention. If they did stop talking after I called them out about it, they would start up again as soon as I started lecturing.

I finally got to the point where I started sending the most incorrigible kids down to see the school disciplinarian with a note explaining why they were being sent to her. I soon learned that this only highlighted my powerlessness because whenever this happened the kid would invariably return within ten minutes with the disciplinarian's signature on the note I prepared. All I really accomplished by doing this was to give the kid a 10-minute recess from class, after which he would return and start the cycle all over again.

Once I almost got into serious trouble when one of the kids started moving his desk to another row in the middle of a class.

"Felipe!" I said. "Stop moving your desk!"

He smiled at me and kept moving the desk.

"Felipe! Put your desk back where it belongs!"

Again the only reaction I got was a smile as he kept sliding his desk across the room.

"*FELIPE!*" I yelled at the top of my lungs. "*I SAID TO STOP MOVING YOUR DESK! ARE YOU DEAF OR JUST STUPID?*"

Suddenly the room became silent. Although I thought I was using a phrase that I had heard used during my school days a thousand times or more, this was apparently the first time my students had heard it.

"Mr. Mike, you can't call Felipe stupid!" one of the girls told me.

"I didn't call him stupid," I said." I asked him which one he was because he wouldn't stop moving his desk, so those were the only two possibilities I could think of to explain why he didn't do what I said."

Of course this was a little bit of a rationalization, since I realized it wasn't the most politically correct way to get his attention, and the kids could probably make it into a major problem for me with their parents if they chose to, but I still believed I wasn't calling the kid stupid. I just wanted to let him know if he had any brains he should do what his teacher told him. So I spent the next 15 minutes trying to explain to the class the difference between calling somebody stupid and asking them to answer the question I posed. It made sense to me that it was a way to get someone to realize they should listen to what they were being told, but I wasn't sure the kids bought it.

However, the bottom line was I really didn't care if they bought it or not. I knew I didn't mean it the way they were trying to make it sound and if they wanted to cause trouble for me over it, so be it. I was getting pretty close to the end of my rope with them anyway, and it wouldn't be long before I actually got there.

This is the type of situation that got repeated every day with the 6th grade classes. For some reason, the 8th and 9th graders that I taught were nowhere near as rowdy or disrespectful. It seemed like the 6th graders were the "bad seeds" of the school.

One day I finally snapped. I guess it had to happen sooner or later. I had just finished teaching a class on one of the English Lit selections the kids were supposed to read when right near the end of the class, one of the girls stood up from her desk and started bouncing and swaying in place, as if she were dancing. I felt like this was just a total slap in my face and I "went off" on her.

"Javiera!" I yelled. "What the hell are you doing?"

She looked at me like I was asking her to explain why she had to breathe. "I was just putting on my sweater", she lied.

"Then what was this?"

I tried to imitate her moves and to my chagrin, this caused gales of laughter to erupt. The kids thought this was hilarious!

After that I lost it. I told them if they thought this was so funny, they could copy 5 pages of their reading books as a punishment. They immediately began whining and complaining, but I told them if they didn't like it they would have 5 more pages to copy. None of this really accomplished anything, but I didn't really know what else to do. Since we were close to the end of the class anyway, I told them that anyone who didn't have it done by the next day would get a zero for the week. (They then reminded me that in Chile, teachers are not allowed to give a zero grade for anything. The lowest grade you can give is a 1 !)

I eventually rescinded the homework assignment after Javiera and another girl from the class visited me in the teachers' conference room afterwards and swore they weren't trying to be disruptive or disrespectful. I told them it was the last time I would go back on a punishment, and I knew it was true because I had already made up my mind that I couldn't teach these kids any more.

I was so frustrated and angry about the lack of control I had with the 6th graders that I emailed my letter of resignation to Monica that night. In addition to the chaos in the classroom and the lack of training or consideration for kids in my classes who spoke no English, the workload was ridiculous for what we were getting paid. Every night I would spend 3 to 4 hours preparing the class lesson plans for each of the subjects I taught for the following day. Adding up the lack of respect from the kids and lack of discipline or support from the school, and I decided I had better leave before I completely lost my temper and said something that would cause more serious problems.

I had intended to stay on a week or so until the school could find another replacement, but Monica found me before I could go to my first class the next day and told me that wouldn't be necessary. She told me that if I truly felt the way I did about the kids in my classes that she could not allow me to continue teaching in the school.

"That's fine with me", I told her. "I have no desire to continue performing as a "toothless tiger" for these kids. I have no way to enforce any discipline with them and they know it. Maybe you can find someone else who can put up with the brats better than me."

This seemed particularly offensive to her.

"They are not *brats!*" she said. "They are very intelligent and creative students. The fact that you can call them that is an insult to the school. I guess you are not intended to be a grade school teacher after all!"

"Maybe not," I said. "But if you remember during our very first Skype interview I told you I never taught kids at this age before and I would need a lot of training and support, which you promised but never provided."

Of course, she didn't see it that way, and we argued back and forth for a few more minutes, but the final result was we both agreed that it was in everybody's best interest that I leave. She told me when I could expect to return to the school to get my final payment and I shook hands and walked back to the apartment.

So ended my brief career as an international school teacher. A new adventure with new challenges was waiting for me just around the bend.

****

Interlude 2

"You know you can't hold me forever
I didn't sign up with you
I'm not a present for your friends to open
This boys too young to be singin'
The Blues"

-Bernie Taupin
Goodbye Yellow Brick Road

"So, do you want to stay or do you want to go?" Yolande is asking me. "It's all up to you."

It's the day before New Year's Eve and my wife has decided it's time to have a confrontation with her siblings. We are sitting in the bedroom of a "bungalow" in a resort park in Holland geared towards families with young children. It's supposed to be a family reunion for Yo, her parents, her brother, sisters, nieces and nephews – and me, of course. It is something they have been doing around the end of the year for the past 3 years, but this is the first time Yo and I have been in Holland during this time of year, so it's the first time we are included. It's supposed to be a place that the whole family can enjoy by staying together in small brick buildings (which are referred to as bungalows by the Dutch) and letting their kids play in the various amusement facilities available, the most obvious of which is a large indoor wading pool where the kids and their parents can "swim" in the dead of winter. It's probably a great place for families with kids under the age of 12 or 13, which describes most of Yolande's siblings' families. However, it quickly turns into something more resembling a prison sentence for me and Yolande and we begin to argue about whether or not we should stay.

It's not so much that the activities available are mostly the type that only kids and their parents can enjoy, it's also the ongoing resentment and frustration I feel whenever I'm involved in the family gatherings. It's not that I don't like them. It's simply because I know very little Dutch, and the rest of Yo's family will only speak Dutch when I'm around, even though they all speak very fluent English. I try to get involved in their conversations as much as I can, but after a while it feels hopeless. No matter how often Yo tries to translate a story or comment one of the others say while we are sitting around the dinner table or anywhere else, the brief discussion in English is quickly followed by long periods of strictly Dutch conversation, leaving me to wonder why I'm even there.

I admit it's mostly my fault. I'm the outsider. I'm the one who still hasn't learned Dutch after my first trip to Holland over 8 years ago. The problem is that I have never stayed in Holland for very long, and even though I have taken a few classes in Dutch back in the U.S., and tried to learn more by using language teaching software, I don't know anyone besides Yolande who speaks it in the U.S., so I don't have much incentive to learn it. On top of that, I've never considered myself a very good student. I've always been a bit of a procrastinator and I almost always had to force myself to study during my student days, so I didn't devote myself to learning the language, especially since there was no real need to do so in America. Unfortunately, this does not lend itself to being assimilated into Yolande's family, who seem to avoid speaking English as much as possible from my perspective.

So, on top of not seeing anything particularly interesting to do for adults in this "bungalow resort" that we've been invited to spend a few days at, I also have to relegate myself to enduring many lengthy conversations from everyone except my wife, but not being able to understand almost any of them. It's definitely not the first time this has happened. It has been this way almost from the first time I met Yo's family in Holland. But now every time I have to sit through a half hour discussion that I have no clue about what's being said, it becomes more and more annoying. It doesn't matter to me if it's intentional or not. It's something I'm tired of having to deal with.

After the first night of our get together, Yolande and I go to the resort's dining room to have breakfast. Although there is food available in the bungalow, there is so much traffic with siblings and kids running in and out, that the restaurant seems preferable for us. While we are having breakfast, my annoyance about having to stay in this environment increases and I become vocal about my irritation at having been put into this situation once again. What sounded like a relatively pleasant diversion from caring for Yo's mother in her home now seems like a 3-day jail sentence, and my frustration grows as I try to discuss it. The fact that my wife isn't exactly sympathetic doesn't really help. By the time we get back to the bungalow we are both in a surly mood, and Yo decides it's time to pull the plug.

She wants to tell her family that she is tired of them ignoring me and only speaking English to me when practically forced to do so, but I tell her I think that will only make things worse. Even though it has been a sore point for a very long time, I don't want to spoil the rest of the family's reunion. However, the fact is that Yo and I can't really see the point of staying in a place that holds almost no interest for either of us. Finally she gives me the ultimatum – decide if you want to stay here and suffer through the next few days with the slight possibility of some enjoyment and camaraderie, or go back to her parent's house and find something to occupy ourselves with there.

It's not an easy decision because I know that leaving will cause some shock waves to ripple through the family, but I can't stand the thought of staying there for the rest of our booking. Reluctantly, I tell her I think its best that we go.

Yo walks out of the bedroom and makes the announcement to her siblings who are all gathered to plan their activities for the day, most of which involve shopping for groceries or taking the kids to the wading pool. As expected, the announcement comes as a total shock to them. They are truly stunned and they all profess that they never realized I was being ignored and didn't deliberately try to exclude me from all of their conversations. I believe them, but I know it will continue to happen again and will always happen until I finally become fluent in Dutch. Besides, it will be almost impossible to stay there now and pretend nothing happened, so we take up Yo's sister's offer to drive us to the train station.

Upon returning to her parent's house, we contact the couple who were planning on coming to the house to feed the cat every day while we were at the bungalow park. They are very surprised that we returned, but immediately invite us to spend New Year's Eve at their home. I have met the husband, named Ton, (but pronounced "Tun"), and know he speaks pretty good English and is very friendly as well. I consider this a vast improvement over the original plan.

On New Year's Eve we go to Ton's house and have a great time with him and his wife. He turns out to love American "oldies" from the 60s, 70s and 80s, and we all take turns "veejaying" music videos on You Tube and singing them as only people who have been drinking all night can.

Right before midnight, his 11 year-old-son comes into the room with enough fireworks to put on a display in Yankee Stadium. We all go outside and watch the annual pyrotechnics that defines the Dutch New Year's Eve celebration. The entire neighborhood comes outside to shoot off firecrackers, rockets, roman candles and God knows what else. The sky is filled with a rainbow of explosions and the bangs and booms continue for well over an hour.

After the fireworks finally start to subside, we go inside for few more drinks before we end the celebration and call it a night. We go outside to get in the car and the streets are so smoky from the fireworks, it looks like we are standing in the middle of a battle field.

Right before we leave, Ton and I give each other a man-hug and he tells me, "I hope you have a better time for the rest of your time in Holland. Don't think Dutch people don't like you if they don't talk to you. Sometimes they don't know what to say."

I think about this and try to think of an intelligent, semi-sober response, but before I can say anything, Ton says "Or maybe they're just stupid!"

We both have a good laugh and give each other one more slap on the back before we leave. As we drive away, I think maybe Ton is right - but considering that I'm the one who is living in a country where he doesn't have a job and can't speak the language, maybe *I'm* the one who's stupid.

After all, there's one thing I should probably know from my experiences in Chile and China.

It's all in the eye of the beholder.

Chile - Part 2

"How does it feel?
To be on your own?
With no direction home?
Like a complete unknown
Like a rolling stone?"

-Bob Dylan
Like a Rolling Stone

After quitting the international school in Antofagasta, I knew it was just a matter of time before the school kicked us out of the apartment. They didn't want to be too pushy about it, however, since Yo was still teaching the third grade class there, and they definitely didn't want to lose *her*. They could survive having one teacher quit, but not two, and they were scared to death that, since Yolande was my wife, and I had decided to quit, that she was planning on doing the same thing soon. Monica had even asked me during my exit interview, "What about Yolande? *She's* not going to quit too, is she?"

It was almost comical to see how much they couldn't care less if I left but they were already getting paranoid about the fact that Yo might leave too. No, I told her. Yolande was not unhappy with her class. She would stay. That gave Monica a little breathing room and also gave us some time before we had to find another place to live.

All that would have to wait, however, until we finished taking our first side trip. The school had a 3-day weekend coming up to celebrate Easter, and we found a perfect weekend trip to fill it in with – the village of San Pedro in the Atacama desert!

Its official name was San Pedro de Atacama, and it was one of the most incredibly beautiful places I'd ever seen. The rocks and sand dunes had the most awesome set of unique colors I could ever have imagined, no less actually have seen. It was only about 4 hours away from Antofagasta, but it felt like we had traveled to another strange, beautiful planet. However, the most fascinating part of the trip was a night astronomy tour.

We hadn't planned on taking the tour, but we got talked into it by two or three of the other members of the tour group we joined for a daytime sightseeing hike through the desert. The landscape was truly awesome, but we hadn't considered the astronomy tour until one of the people in our group told us how great it would be to see the stars and constellations in the world's clearest sky.

He was definitely right. The Atacama Desert is the world's driest desert and one of the highest deserts in the world. As a result, there are very, very few nights when there are any clouds in the sky. Astronomers come there from all over the world to study the stars and the planets through extremely powerful telescopes. We went on the nighttime tour and were extremely glad we did.

One of the bonuses from taking this tour was that it was led by a Canadian astronomer who had relocated to Chile specifically to study and work in observatories in the Atacama. After an hour or so of pointing out various constellations and letting us see some of the more prominent stars and planets through outdoor telescopes, we gathered inside a shelter building to discuss the observations over hot chocolate.

One of the things the astronomer talked about was something called the ALMA project. I had never heard of this before, but the more he told us about it, the more fascinating it became. The actual name of the project is the Atacama Large Millimeter/submillimeter Array and it's basically a network of 66 giant mobile telescopes that can see light waves thousands and thousands of miles into space - so far in fact, that they can pick up the light waves that created some stars millions of years ago. Since I'm not a scientist or an astronomer, the ideas he was talking about were almost too advanced for me to even understand, but what I did understand was amazing.

The whole trip was so incredibly beautiful and fascinating that Yo and I hated to leave to go back to Antofagasta. But you have to face the real world sometime, so when the three days were over, we headed back on the bus to the city.

Since I had quit the international school, I had to find something else to do, but I already knew I would be able to get a job as an English instructor at one of the English language schools in town. In fact, Kurt, who along with Amy, had been our roommate for two weeks when we first arrived, had been working there for a few weeks and he recruited me even before my fateful afternoon with the 6th graders. "All you have to is call Manuel and tell him you're ready," he said.

Manuel was the owner and hiring manager for The King's Language Institute in town. It was a short bus ride from the new apartment we found after moving out of the one we had originally been in, and the hourly rate wasn't too bad. When I met Manuel he seemed like a fairly relaxed, friendly man in his early 40s who was very determined to have native English speakers on his staff to enhance the reputation of his school. I went into his office for an interview, and he guaranteed to pay me for 20 hours per week, no matter how many hours I actually worked. On top of that, Kurt had already told me that the classes were extremely easy. In fact, he even told me he hardly ever used the textbook and simply had conversations with his advanced students in English.

"Don't you have to use the textbook for grammar and stuff?" I asked him.

"Haven't had to so far", he said.

"Well, what do you talk about for two hours (the normal class length)?"

"Whatever they want to talk about", Kurt replied.

"Man." I said. "I don't think I've ever talked to anyone for two hours in my life!"

Kurt laughed and said "I guess that's one of the benefits of my having been a bartender in Kansas City for so many years. You have to find ways to talk to people and make it entertaining."

I was scheduled to sit in on one of Kurt's classes as part of my training before I started teaching real students, so I was eager to watch and see just how he did it. Amazingly enough, on the day I sat in on one of his classes with a young college-age girl, he worked almost exclusively with the textbook that he told me he almost never used! When I asked him why he did this after the class was over he said "Well, I guess I use the textbook sometimes if they (the students) don't want to talk much. It really depends on them." I remember thinking this explanation seemed somewhat over simplified, but I thought, "Hey, if it works for him, I guess it'll work for me".

Well, I don't know if I was just not as creative or talented as Kurt when it came to conversation, but I soon found out that I couldn't simply talk my way through most of the two-hour class sessions I taught, and that most of the time I *had* to use the book, or else the student and I would simply be sitting and staring at each other.

Occasionally I had a student who seemed to enjoy simply speaking English and asking me questions about life in America and other places I'd visited, but for the most part, we had to go by the book. Besides, I actually felt a little guilty if I didn't use the textbook for most of the lessons, like I was cheating the student out of a real lesson. Kurt didn't see it that way, but I decided I had to find the right style for me, and it had to be a mixture of the textbook for grammar and conversation for fun.

I actually seemed to have some success with this approach and I began picking up more class hours as a last-minute substitute for other teachers who got sick, and eventually got my own set of students that I was the regular instructor for each week. However, the student clientele was always changing, as some of them basically completed the advanced classes, some of them were promoted to other jobs in new locations and some of them simply stopped coming for whatever reason. Since I got paid for no-shows, I really didn't mind if someone didn't show up for his or her class, as long as I still got paid. In spite of all this, I still wasn't getting more than 13 or 14 hours of classes per week, which Manuel wasn't too happy about since he still had to pay me for 20.

After about a month or so, Manuel came up with a solution. He would send me to teach at the Tesoro copper mine for two days each week, and schedule me to have 8 classes per day, so I would definitely have over 20 hours of classes each week. This was fine with me too, since I got paid for any hours in excess of 20 hours as well. Besides, traveling to a copper mine and staying overnight each week sounded a little more interesting that sitting in a classroom. So I agreed to make the weekly trip.

Prior to being allowed to travel to the mine, I had to go to a safety briefing at a small one-story building not far from the King's Language offices. I didn't know why I had to go, since I obviously wouldn't be going into the mine itself, but Manuel told me it was a requirement that had to be fulfilled. So I proceeded to the address I had been given and waited, along with about 20 other men, outside a small, graffiti covered one story garage type building for someone to open a padlocked chain link fence gate.

After a few minutes, one of the men came over to me and asked "Are you Michael?" I answered that I was and then he introduced himself to me as Fernando Leal, and that he was also attending the safety briefing because he too was a new hire for The King's Language who needed to be qualified to teach English at the mine.

He didn't look like an American or Brit, or any type of native English speaker, so I asked him where he was from. "Canada", he said. It was interesting how many foreign English teachers in Chile came from Canada. In his case, it was even more unusual because he was Chilean by birth, but he had moved to Canada as a kid and eventually came back to Chile. Manuel had sent him to the briefing with instructions to not only fulfill the mine's requirements, but to also interpret them for me.

Once the gate was opened, we all filed into a small room with folding chairs and a projection screen at the front of the room. Fernando sat next to me and started to explain to me in English what the narrator of the safety film was saying in Spanish. For a short time he was telling me "This is all background information about the company", and "This is just general information about why safety is important in the mines and that there is a lot of danger when you work in a mine."

So far he wasn't really telling me anything I couldn't figure out on my own. However, he knew part of his duty was to explain what was happening and being said on the screen, so he continued to translate some of the obvious warnings from the film. If a sequence appeared on the screen showing somebody bumping his head on a low ceiling or protruding beam, etc. and then wearing a safety helmet to prevent anything like that happening again, Fernando would lean over to me and whisper "This is saying that you should always wear a hard hat in the mine, because it's easy to get hurt by bumping your head against something." Likewise, if the video showed someone dropping something heavy on his foot and yelling in pain, followed by the same person putting on a pair of safety shoes to guard against a reoccurrence of this type of accident, he would tell me "This is supposed to show you why it's important to wear safety shoes in the mine." Everything the safety film showed was so obvious that after a few minutes, Fernando just stopped explaining to me by saying "This is all stuff about what you have to do when you go down into the mine. We won't be doing that, so none of this is anything we need to know." I was sure he was right, so we watched the rest of the 15-minute video in silence, just like the rest of the audience. The only difference was they probably *did* need to know what was on the video, as they all looked like the type of laborers who made their living working in mines.

After about an hour, Fernando and I had finished step one of our qualifications to teach English at the mine. The next step was to get a physical from doctors who were authorized by the mining company to certify that we were healthy enough to travel to the mine location, especially since it required us to live at an altitude of over 3000 meters above sea level. Yolande and I had already been to Lake Titicaca in Peru, which was over 3800 meters above sea level, so I was sure I wouldn't have a problem. However, since I spoke almost no Spanish, Fernando was once again assigned to guide me through the process.

We had a series of examinations to go through including hearing tests, vision tests and the usual heart and breathing check with a stethoscope, etc. Each one of these was administered by a different doctor at a clinic with at least 30 other patients waiting to go through the same procedures. However, instead of calling out our names individually, as they did for all the other patients, the nurses and clerks called out both of our names and we had to go through each examination together. I felt like we were being announced as a comedy team, or a dance team every time one of the clerks or nurses called out *"Fernando Leal and Michael Durack"*. The only thing that was missing was the phrase *"Direct from Las Vegas"* followed by thunderous applause.

Although the doctors had some qualms about certifying me as fit for teaching English in the mine because I had had a collapsed lung that required surgery to correct 30 years earlier, they eventually rated me as qualified to venture into the mining environs at 3000 meters above sea level. Fernando was almost disqualified also due to his being slightly overweight, but in the end, he was certified as well. We were finally ready to enlighten the Tesoro mine company managers in their quest to learn more perfect English.

Manuel told me where to catch the bus that would pick me up on Monday morning and take me on the 3-hour trip to the mine in the wilds of the desert. There I would conduct 7 or 8 classes, and then stay overnight in one of the mining company's barracks, teach another 7 or 8 classes the following day, and return to Antofagasta, again by company bus. So the next Monday, I packed my laptop and my overnight bag, took the elevator down to the street and walked to the main road to wait for my bus which was supposed to arrive at 5:45 a.m.

I waited in the dark and wondered how I could recognize the bus that was supposed to take me to the mine. Graciela, one of the other teachers from The Kings Language who was also going to the mine, told me the day before that it was a big Pullman bus, which was a large, commercial tour bus similar to a Greyhound bus in the U.S. Graciela wasn't sure if it would have any markings on it that indicated it was going to the Tesoro mine, which I thought was strange since she had been taking this bus each week for months. However, she assured me that it would stop at the right place where I was waiting and the driver would tell me it was the right bus.

It all sounded pretty simple, but now that I was standing in the dark watching several different tour busses zoom by, I was getting nervous and worried that I wouldn't know which bus I was supposed to take. I had been standing at the designated bus stop since 5:30 to make sure I didn't miss it if it came by a little early. By 5:55 am it still hadn't arrived and now I was really worried I had missed it. I called Graciela on my cell phone to try to find out if she knew if there was any problem with the bus schedule, but of course, there was no answer.

Finally, around 6:10 a.m., a large tour bus slowed down and pulled over to a stop in front of the shelter I was waiting at, along with 2 other men. Lo and behold, the electric display on the front window *did* say "Tesoro", so I was pretty sure this had to be the right one.

When I got on the bus, I had to give my passport to a young man who functioned as the driver's assistant. I don't think they have a comparable position on the Greyhound busses in America, at least not on the ones that I've traveled on. The bus was actually quite a bit different than any I had been on in the U.S. also. It was very long and roomy, with plenty of comfortable seats available. On top of that, I was the only person on the bus besides one man who was sleeping in a seat way towards the back. The attendant gave me a pillow and a blanket, just like you get on longer flights in America, and I picked out a seat.

The bus made several stops as we passed through Antofagasta, taking on more passengers each time, most of them men who immediately plopped down into a seat and went to sleep. I started getting nervous again because I still didn't see Graciela and it made me wonder if I was actually on the right bus. Finally, I saw a woman who looked a little like Graciela with a winter hat and sunglasses get on near the front of the bus and promptly drop into one of the seats closer to the front. I had deliberately left an open seat next to me so that she could sit next to me if she wanted, and we could socialize to some extent during our 3-hour trip to the mine. Since she never even looked to see if I was on the bus, I assumed she wasn't interested in any social conversation. I closed my eyes and tried to fall asleep, but after a few minutes realized that wasn't going to happen.

I didn't have any books or magazines to read because there was no place to get anything printed in English in Antofagasta, so I basically had to sit in my seat, listening to the other passengers snoring, and tried to pass the time by singing songs to myself or trying to imagine future stories I might be able to write. It wasn't even possible to look out the windows since all the other passengers seemed to want to keep the curtains closed so they could catch an hour or two of sleep on their way to the mine. All the while I kept wondering if I was on the right bus and what I would be able to do if it turned out I wasn't.

After about 2 and ½ hours the bus slowed down and I risked pushing the curtain aside slightly enough to try to see where we were. I saw what looked like a small town with a few shabby looking general stores along either side of the street, and even shabbier looking small gray brick and cinder block buildings with small dirt yards surrounded by concrete or adobe walls decorated with various graffiti. I assume we must be arriving at the town where the mine was located, but as the bus kept going, I realized I was wrong. It was actually a small desert town called Sierra Gorda, and as I looked at it through the bus window, I had to wonder how anyone or anything could stand living in such an isolated barren environment.

After another half hour or so, we stopped at a crossing gate like the ones used for railroad crossings with a small brick building next to it on the side of the road. There were three or four people inside dressed in some kind of uniform, and I assumed they were security guards. The bus driver's assistant who had taken my passport about 3 hours earlier stepped off the bus and disappeared into the brick building.

He was gone for at least 15 minutes and when he finally returned he walked up the steps onto the bus and called out "Michael Durack?"

Dammit! Now I was going to have to answer some questions which I probably wouldn't understand and it had to have something to do with the fact that I had a foreign passport. I walked towards the front of the bus and just as I was about to go through the door, I saw Fernando sitting in one of the front seats. He got up from his seat and said "I'll come with you."

We walked up to the window of the brick building where one of the women security guards started asking me something in Spanish, which I didn't understand a word of, but luckily Fernando did and he answered the questions for me. The security guard must have been satisfied with his answers because she gave him back my passport and he handed it to me.

As we turned around to get back on the bus, I saw Graciela standing there, almost unrecognizable in her heavy winter coat, scarf wrapped around her face, sunglasses and winter stocking cap pulled down around her ears. It *was* pretty cold during the mornings there, but I thought this was carrying things a bit too far.

"What did they want?" she asked Fernando.

"Ah, they just didn't know who he was. I told them he was with us."

I wondered why they didn't know who I was since the arrangements were supposedly all made long before we came to the mine, and why they seemed to know who Fernando and Graciela were, but not me, since we were all representing the same language school. I also wondered why I hadn't been able to find either Graciela or Fernando on the bus, and why they obviously hadn't made any effort to see if I was there, but I kept all these questions to myself as we got back on the bus and continued the journey to the mine.

Once we passed the gate, it was just a matter of minutes before we pulled into the parking lot of a fairly large one story building they called the *casino*, but which I would call the mess hall, since it looked like the one I used to go to when I was in Boy Scout camp many years before.

As we got off the bus and collected our luggage, I mentioned to Graciela "I didn't even see you on the bus!"

"Yeah," she answered "I just go to sleep as soon as I get on."

Some team leader, I thought to myself. Shouldn't she at least know if the whole team was there?

"Do you know where I have to go for the first class?" I asked her.

"Yes, but you can have breakfast first," she said. "All the meals are free here."

Well, okay, but it was already nearly 10 minutes before 9:00 am and my first class was supposed to start at 9:00.

"You can start a little later because it is the first day today, but you should try to be ready by 9:15."

Okay, fine by me, let's go, I told her. She and Fernando led the way into the mess hall where you had to give your passport to a woman sitting behind a glass window. The woman than passed each person's passport over a bar scanning window and the bar code from a sticker on the passport beeped as a red light flashed. The process seemed to work fine for Graciela and Fernando, but of course it wouldn't beep for me, even though I had stuck the label with the bar code that the school had given me on the back of my passport, just as I had been told. It took another few minutes of explanations from Graciela in Spanish before the woman behind the window would let me pass through.

Once inside the mess hall I followed Graciela and Fernando through the cafeteria-style line and found a table to eat with them. We had a very quick conversation about what to expect as we all wolfed down the fruit, pancakes and scrambled eggs we had been provided (none of it being the kind of breakfast you would ever want to eat if you had a choice). Then, Graciela said "Let's go!" and I followed her to the main administration building about 400 yards away.

It was a two story T- shaped building with a large expanded square in the center where all three wings connected. This was the reception area with a large square shaped counter in the center of the room and seating along all four walls. There were two to three receptionists inside the counter square at any given time, talking on the phone or answering questions from visitors. There were always dozens of people walking into, out of and through this area and it took Graciela a few minutes to get one of the receptionists to tell her where all the offices were that I was going to teach that day.

It turned out that my first class was supposed to be with a manager who wasn't even there that day. He had gotten an extra day off for some reason, so he would not arrive until the next day. So Graciela spent the next half hour walking me around to all the offices I would have to give my lessons in, including two in another building approximately another 300 yards down the road. Aside from the somewhat lax orientation procedure I had gone through in the morning, the rest of the day was pretty uneventful and much less stressful.

The managers I was assigned to teach were, without exception, friendly and eager to learn. I later found out that one of the reasons for this was that it was a requirement they had to fulfill in order to collect all of their year-end bonus money. Still, after the first day, I was able to find all my classes on my own and follow the class schedule on a routine basis.

After the last class, around 8:00 pm, Graciela, Fernando and I met for dinner in the mess hall. The food was free, and we got three meals a day, but the bad news was that it was just barely preferable to not eating at all. Still, it could have been worse, and after dinner Graciela gave Fernando and me the keys to our rooms.

The rooms we stayed in overnight were basically one of the barracks type accommodations that the mine provided for its regular employees. Due to the fact that most workers either worked on a Monday through Thursday or a Friday through Sunday schedule, there were always empty rooms available for visitors like us. They were just big enough for one person, but they had a bed, a flat screen TV with satellite programming, a shared bathroom with the next barracks room, and a portable heater. The last item was especially important because after the sun went down in the desert, the temperature dropped well below freezing and the wind often blew across the open desert with a vengeance.

The next morning I met Graciela and Fernando in the mess hall for breakfast and repeated the lesson schedule from the day before. The day went along very routinely. The only difference from the day before is that some of the managers would have to cancel their classes due to urgent work requirements. Other than that, there wasn't any trauma at all, and Graciela, Fernando and I met in the reception area after our last class for the return trip home, by taxi this time because there weren't enough people leaving the mine after two days to make it practical for the tour bus company to schedule a bus for the return trip.

For the next two or three weeks, everything seemed to be running along fine without any stress or drama. Then for some reason, everything changed sometime during the third or fourth week.

****

I'm not the kind of person who automatically becomes your best friend from the moment I meet you. I like to think I'm fairly easy going and pretty flexible most of the time, but I know it takes me a while to warm up to people. My friends seem to think I'm very funny and I was known as a "comedian" in high school and college and to many of my co-workers as well. Still, I tend to hang back quietly when I first meet new people and at times it seems that some of them take that the wrong way. My wife says I sometimes appear "unapproachable" or uninterested in talking to other people (which, I admit, is usually true), so I tend to give off "bad vibes". Still, no matter where I go in the world, it seems that I'm always the first one a beggar will pick out of a crowd of people to ask for money. Even worse, I usually feel sorry for anyone who has to resort to something like this, so I almost always give them something. I often wonder why I don't seem unapproachable or give off "bad vibes" to people who want money!

Anyway, this is the only explanation I can come up with to explain the behavior that Fernando and Graciela showed towards me starting around the fourth week of going to the mine.

We had all finished our classes for the day on a Monday evening and gathered together to go to the mess hall for dinner, as we always did. We had gotten fairly familiar with each other by this time, and the conversations were fairly easy. Graciela and Fernando were both very fluent in English (obviously, since they were teaching English, just like me), and from my point of view we all seemed to get along well and usually had relatively pleasant discussions during our meals together.

At the end of our dinner conversations that evening, I asked if we should plan on meeting for breakfast the next morning. My first class started at 9:00 a.m., so I asked if we should meet in front of the mess hall around 8:30.

"No", Fernando told me. "I have a class at 8:00 tomorrow."

"Yeah, me too," said Graciela.

Okay, I told them I would just have to have breakfast by myself. I certainly wasn't willing to get up an hour earlier than necessary just to meet them for breakfast. We all left the mess hall together and said goodnight before we went off to our separate rooms.

The next morning I went to the mess hall around 8:30 to eat the almost edible food they served before I started my first class. While I was collecting my food from the serving counter, I looked out into the dining area and was surprised at what I saw. There was Fernando and Graciela sitting together at one of the tables!

I finished picking out the eggs, rolls and fruit juice from the cafeteria line I thought I could possibly eat and walked over to sit down with them.

"I thought you both had a class at 8:00?" I said.

"Yeah, but they got cancelled", Fernando said.

"They got cancelled?" I asked "How did you know?"

"Our students sent Graciela an email last night. She got it when she got back to the room and she called me and told me", he said.

I thought it was strange that neither one of them would call me to let me know, but before I could say much about it, they both decided it was time to get up and leave. They had obviously finished their breakfast, but it still seemed like a quick exit to me.

I told myself it was all in my head and walked off to the first class once I had finished my breakfast. I decided not to make a big deal out of it and that it was probably nothing more than a little thoughtlessness on their part.

However, when I came to the reception area after my 11:00 am class, as I usually did to meet Graciella and Fernando before we all went to the mess hall for lunch, they weren't there. I waited a good fifteen minutes and when they still didn't show up, I walked over on my own.

I was sitting at a table, halfway through my lunch when they both walked in. I finished eating as they went through the cafeteria line, and even though I knew they saw me, they walked over and sat at a different table on the other side of the room.

By this time I was getting pretty steamed. I wasn't going to pretend I didn't know what they were doing, even if I didn't understand why they were doing it. I didn't know what I could have done to be "shunned" by my co-workers, but by this time, I didn't really care.

I walked over to where they were sitting and told them, straight out, "Look, if you don't want to sit at the same table with me, that's fine. From now on, I'll come here on my own and eat by myself and I won't bother asking you if you want to join me or not."

Graciella looked surprised, but Fernando suddenly became combative.

"What are you doing? What is this, kindergarten?" he asked. "Do we have to act like babies?"

"You tell me," I told him. "You're the ones who want to stay away from me for some reason."

"Oh, this is ridiculous! Go on! Go stay by yourself, if that's what you want! Go on!"

I walked away from the table, still trying to figure out what caused this sudden hostility, but I certainly wasn't going to beg them to let me eat with them. I would just have to work on my own from then on for the two days I was at the mine each week.

I thought that over time, things would change and we would resume being friendly and sharing meals together, but it never happened. For some reason, they both continued giving me the cold shoulder for the rest of the time I taught lessons there. This made for some really frosty rides back to Antofagasta when we would return by taxi on the second night, with both of them sitting in the back seat while I sat in the front. During the 2 and ½ hours it took to complete the trip, they had extensive conversations in Spanish, which they knew I wouldn't understand, and only spoke English to me to say goodbye when they got to their stop.

This lasted for about another 4 weeks, at which time Yolande's classes at the international school went on a two-week semester break, so we took the opportunity to travel to Peru. When I returned, I was told I would no longer be on the weekly mine assignment. Manuel told me there had been some complaints from one of the students I taught, and I would have to meet with *Graciela* to discuss the details!

I had no choice but to agree and I met Graciela at the school office in Antofagasta, where she was as vague and mysterious as possible while telling me that one of the students wanted a different teacher for his lessons. She asked me if I had any problems with any of the students and I said no. She asked me if I was too rigid about going by the book to teach my lessons and not allowing enough time for conversations (which was supposedly one of the complaints against me). I told her no, that in fact I always thought that it was just the opposite – that perhaps I might be spending too much time on conversations and not enough time on the text book lessons. In fact, there was only one student I could think of that I always went through the two pages of each lesson with, and only then because he *insisted* that we cover every exercise in every chapter. Other than that I spent a good deal of time talking to each student about their jobs, their families and their favorite activities when they weren't working at the mine. Graciela just shook her head and said she didn't know why someone had made the complaints and that sometimes the students were hard to figure out, but I knew it was all bullshit. She and Fernando had obviously decided while I was gone on my trip that they would find some way to get me reassigned, and they either talked one of the students into making a "complaint", or more likely, they just made up the whole thing on their own.

In either case, I didn't really care. By this time, I was actually tired of making the trip each week and could easily live without getting up at 5:00 a.m. to catch the bus to the mine every Monday morning, trying unsuccessfully to sleep during the 3-hour trip, the really bad food while I was there, and being conspicuously ignored during the frosty ride home in the taxi each Tuesday evening. Besides, I was still guaranteed 20 hours of class fees each week, regardless of how many hours I actually taught, so getting paid almost as much for working less hours was fine with me.

So after approximately 10 weeks, my teaching career at the world's second largest copper mine was over. I never got to see the actual mine, and it definitely wasn't all fun, but it was interesting enough while it lasted.

Actually, now that I'm looking back on them, I can probably say the same thing about all our travel experiences: whether they were all fun or not, they *were* all interesting enough while they lasted.

I kept teaching at The Kings Language Institute for a few more months, but without the mine classes each week, my total hours dropped way down below 20. I knew it was just a matter of time before Manuel would terminate his 20 hour guarantee. But as long as I was getting paid for a minimum of 20 hours per week, no matter how many I actually taught, it was worthwhile to stay there. The only problem was that Manuel was always at least a month behind in his wage payments.

Sometimes he would pay me a third of what he owed me and promised to pay the balance within the next week. Other times he would pay the full amount, but only after I had to wait another week or so. He never, ever paid the full amount due on time, and he didn't pay anything at all unless you pushed him for it.

Some of the teachers didn't seem to mind it. Kurt, who was the one who told me about working there in the first place, never asked for his pay, and as a result his wages were always over 2 months past due. Another American teacher at the school told me he had worked there for 11 years and it had *always* been that way. I asked him why he had stayed there so long, but he told me he was receiving a good pension from his former employer in the states and it didn't create any financial problems for him. It didn't create any significant problems for me either, since Yolande was working at the international school and getting paid on time every two weeks, but I still wasn't happy about having to wait a month or longer to get paid.

****

After checking into some of the other English language schools in town, I was able to find another position teaching for a school that *always* paid on time and gave much more support than I had received at either the international school or at The King's Language Institute. So I finally walked into Manuel's office one day and told him it was time to pull the plug. I thought he would be angry, but he actually asked me what my future plans were, and when I told him my wife's contract at the international school was over by next March, he asked me if I wanted to come back and help him manage a new branch school he wanted to open in Santiago!

I told him I'd think about it, but internally I said to myself "Oh, yeah! I'd love to get on this merry-go-round again and have to beat on your desk every time I was supposed to get paid. Right! I may be stupid at times, but I'm not *that* stupid!"

Meanwhile, Yolande was still teaching her third grade class at the international school, and she was having her own share of challenges there. She was one of three third grade teachers, and all three of them were supposed to have weekly meetings to plan how they would cover their subjects during the coming week, and also how to implement a new "cutting edge" teaching philosophy called the "PYP" program. The other two teachers were younger than Yo, one of them just a year or two out of college, and neither of them wanted to participate in the PYP program.

One of them, an American named Samantha, was a "by the book" teacher who was paranoid about trying to teach without being tied to a textbook, as the PYP program advocated. She would literally have panic attacks when she tried to address how to teach her class using the PYP concepts which were intended to be more student oriented and integrate all subject areas with a comprehensive teaching approach. The other third grade teacher was also an American, but more importantly, she was basically an overgrown college girl and also a borderline alcoholic who regularly came to school on Friday mornings hung over or semi-drunk from partying all night at the local disco the night before.

During their weekly meetings, all three third grade teachers were supposed to plan their classes for the week as a team. However, it soon became evident to Yolande that neither of them had any intention of trying to work together and resisted any efforts Yo made to try to follow the program they were told to use. After weeks of trying to persuade them that it was possible to meet the objectives of the PYP program, Yo basically gave up and simply went through the motions at the meetings.

On top of that, it also became obvious that the school really had no intention of trying to insure that the students received the best education possible, even though their parents were paying one of the steepest tuitions in the city. Their main goal was simply to make money. The PYP program that they officially endorsed and the native English-speaking teachers were all just for show to justify the tuition they charged. The only thing that kept us there after the school year ended in December was the fact that Yo would have almost a two-month vacation period that she would be paid for upon her return at the beginning of the new school year in March.

Vacation time was *travel* time for us, and we took advantage of the time off to take relatively cheap trips to Peru, Ecuador and the southern half of Chile. The end result was, just like in China, the real benefit of being a foreign English teacher in Chile was the opportunity to travel to other places. It *almost* made up for all the aggravation that came with the teaching part. But even if it didn't make up for all of it, it was an experience we never could have had any other way, so despite all the problems and frustrations we had to go through, in the end we were still glad we did it.

****

Peru

"I see skies of blue
And clouds of white
The bright blessed day,
The dark sacred night
And I think to myself
What a wonderful world"

-Bob Thiele, George David- Weiss
What a Wonderful World

The first place we went on Yolande's first two week break after the end of her first semester was Peru. There were several places we went to that were beautiful and interesting during our stay in South America, but the most exciting one was the Nazca Lines.

I had never heard of them until we went to Chile, but the Nazca Lines were strange, hieroglyphic-like trenches, carved into the earth in the northern edge of the Atacama Desert, which were so large and in such an isolated area that they could only be seen from the air. The way one did this was to book a flight on a small 7 passenger propeller driven airplane and swoop over the 9 or 10 amazing "crop circle" pictures in the earth and wonder who would have made the effort to create such organic artwork – and why.

The official name for these designs are *geoglyphs* and archeologists estimate that they are around 1500 years old or more, and that they were made by the ancient Nazca people who lived there then. Some of them are just a series of simple lines but several of them are definitely designs of animals like fish, spiders, birds, monkeys, etc. and also flowers, trees and plants. The largest ones are over 600 feet across. Some people believed they were made in honor of, or under the direction of visitors from other planets. It seemed like a plausible explanation, given the fact that airplanes weren't invented for nearly 1900 years later, and the only way to see them is from a few hundred feet up. Plus, one of the designs on the side of a hill looks like a cartoon-like human figure in an astronaut's suit.

Other people believed they had some type of religious significance. Whatever caused them, they were undeniably a "must see" attraction.

We boarded the small twin propeller plane along with a young Japanese couple, our pilot and a guide. The wife in the other couple was already acting nervous as we stood on the tarmac, waiting to board the tiny plane.

"Don't worry," the pilot told her as he opened the cabin doors. "It won't take too long!" as if she were about to undergo some type of medical procedure instead of an exciting vacation experience. This didn't seem to calm her down very much, but her husband kept mumbling something to her in Japanese and finally was able to coax her onto the plane.

Once we were in the air, we flew for about 5 minutes over the barren desert, looking down on what seemed like a sea of brown rocks and dirt. Suddenly, we saw the first hieroglyphic symbol – the "Spider".

It was amazing to see something that large, that was created so long ago and could only be seen from the air. The pilot swooped low over it, and then banked sharply to the right so we could fly over it again and take more pictures. After two or three passes, the pilot flew on to the next symbol and performed the same aerobatic maneuvers, swooping low and then banking to return and fly over the same spot a second and third time to make sure all his passengers had a chance to memorialize their flight. He continued performing aerial acrobatics this way over about a dozen different symbols, each one more interesting than the last.

It was really exciting and awesome at the same time – so much so, that the plane's continuous swoops and banking didn't bother me at all. But I soon found out Yo didn't have the exact same experience. Although she too was mesmerized by the site of the mysterious symbols below, her stomach did not adapt to the twisting, turning motions of the plane and I heard her reach for the barf bag that was conveniently provided for just such an occasion.

But it didn't stop her for long! As soon as she finished barfing, she put the bag down and continued to take more pictures of each one of the geoglyphs we flew over. When it was done after about 30 minutes, we all got off the plane and noticed that Yo wasn't the only one who needed the paper sack. The wife of the Japanese couple was also holding one behind her back, hoping no one would notice.

"Don't feel bad," Yo told her, laughing. Then she held up her own bag and said "Look, I've got one too!"

That seemed to do the trick as we all started laughing together. The bottom line was we had just seen one of the most awesome and interesting ancient mysteries on the planet, and we had pictures to prove it. So what if you had to lose your breakfast to see it?

There were a lot of places in Peru that were really cool to see. One of them was Lake Titicaca, the highest lake in the world, and the name that always made me laugh out loud in my 5th grade geography class. Before we left on our trip we were advised to buy some pills to take in case of altitude sickness, since we would be traveling by bus to stay overnight in a town located over 3800 meters, or over 12,000 feet above sea level, and some people seem to have bad reactions to being that high on the planet.

We both took the pills before we left, although Yo never seemed to suffer any effects from the altitude at all. I did have a headache that night, however that kept me from getting much sleep. Aside from that neither of us had much of a reaction. The next day we took a boat cruise on the lake and stopped at an island village made entirely from floating reeds. The local people who lived on this floating island welcomed tourists who docked there and bought some of their handmade clothes, which were very bright and colorful, and other souvenirs.

After docking on the island for an hour or so, we continued on to a non-floating island called Amantani. Amatani had no vehicles on it, and it was populated by several families that took in tourists to stay with them overnight. The highlight of the trip was a hike to the top of one of the two small mountains on the island called "Pachamama" for some awesome sunset views of Titicaca.

When we arrived at the dock, we were greeted by a group of about 15 women dressed in colorful native clothing. Each one of them had a group of tourists assigned to them, usually a couple or small family, and they led them up the steep hillside to the home they would be staying in.

Our hostess led us up the hill to her home where she lived with her father and two young sons. Although she spoke no English and we spoke little Spanish, we were able to communicate fairly well. It was a pretty interesting way to experience life like one of the locals without actually living it every day.

She served us lunch and afterwards we gathered for the hike up to the top of Pachamama. Our guide had warned us it would be a little steep, and he definitely wasn't kidding. I'm not particularly good at uphill hiking, especially *steep* uphill hiking, so I was one of the slowest members in our group making the climb. There was one other woman who was actually slower than me, and I tried to stay close to her to give her moral support until she finally gave up and decided to return to the home where she was staying that night. After that I officially became the slowest member of the party to make the climb, and the last one to reach the summit, just before the last 2 or 3 minutes of sundown. Yo had gone on ahead of me and beat me to the top by a good 15 minutes or so, which was just enough time to snap a few good pictures of the sunset.

That night, we were all supposed to attend a party in the town square that the locals arranged for the tourists. Everyone was supposed to wear some native clothing, supplied by the host families and go into town for more authentic local food and drinks. Before it was time to leave, however, I developed a case of "the shakes". On rare occasions, when I'm tired or not feeling well, I get violent shivers that seem to take over my body for a while. It has only happened 3 or 4 times in my life, and it usually goes away if I can get myself covered up well enough to stay warm, but even then it can last for an hour or more. Well, this was one of those nights. The high altitude might have had something to do with it, but the bottom line was I had to stay in bed, covered by thick woolen blankets to keep me from shaking myself to death. Yo had to dress up in the native women's costume and go the party with our host's ancient looking father. She didn't really mind, and based on some of the pictures she had taken at the party that night, had a relatively good time.

The only other less than pleasant experience we had during our stay on the island was going to the bathroom at night. The house we were staying in did not have a bathroom inside, so you had to go out the bedroom door and down some steps to get to the brick outhouse in the back yard. It wasn't that long of a walk, but the problem was that the temperature dropped below freezing at night due to the high altitude, so before you left you had to get fully dressed with socks, shoes and a coat or jacket if you didn't want to freeze your ass off on the way to the outhouse. Needless to say, this became a desperate race to get dressed in time if you had to answer an urgent call in the middle of the night, so we tried to keep these trips to a minimum. However, we both got to enjoy the experience at least once during the night.

The absolute highlight of our entire Peruvian trip was to visit the ruins of the ancient Inca city of Macchu Picchu. The pictures that everyone has seen of it don't do it justice. It is truly an amazing place to visit and I recommend that anyone who ever has an opportunity to go there should take it. It's worth it just to see the llamas that roam all over the place, pushing tourists aside who might happen to be on the steps or pathways they want to walk through! On top of that, it's one of the greatest places in the world for shutter bugs like us.

****

Ecuador

"Here comes the sun
Here comes the sun
And I say
It's alright!"

-George Harrison
Here Comes The Sun

The next place we went to during Yolande's second semester break was Ecuador. I didn't know much about Ecuador except that it was in South America, but Yo said it sounded like a good place to visit, and it would include 4 nights in tourists' jungle huts in a section of the Amazon rain forest, so I said "Let's go!"

We flew to Guayaquil and took a bus from there to get to the town where we would meet our guide and continue on to the mini-resort in the jungle. We waited in the restaurant that our instructions told us to go to and waited for our guide to appear. After about a half hour, a very serious young man named Juan spotted us sitting at one of the outdoor tables and came over to introduce himself. He asked us if we had all the supplies we had been instructed to bring with us on the checklist we received online. I told him the only thing we didn't have were sandals.

"You'd better get them," he said. "You're going to need them". I went off to search the stores on either side of the street we were on to try to find a reasonable pair of sandals. Unfortunately, because it was only 8:30 or so in the morning, not many places were open. I finally found a suitable pair for both me and Yo and went off to change clothes in the restaurant bathroom. Juan had told us we had to change into our bathing suits and sandals because part of our journey would require us to paddle a large canoe down the river to or resort. It took a while because there was only one bathroom for all 11 of us to use, but eventually everyone got changed and was ready to go. We all piled into a bus and rode for another 45 minutes to the river where our canoe was waiting.

As usual, Yo and I were the oldest members of our group. Besides us, there was an American girl, an Australian, two German girls, a Brit, and two German couples, all of them no older than 30, and most of them much younger. We didn't have much to say to each other on the bus, but when we got to the river, we stopped for a picnic lunch near the town of Nueva Loja where we would continue the journey by canoe and were able to make a few introductions.

After lunch we all got into the large, 12 seat canoe with Juan at the front, giving directions as we headed off down the river. We all had our bathing suits and sandals on, as Juan had instructed, and also rain ponchos, since he had assured us "there will be rain" before we reached our destination.

He was right! Halfway down the river the clouds suddenly darkened and within seconds we were drenched by a mid-day downpour. It didn't last longer than a half an hour or so, but by then we realized why Juan wanted to make sure we had all changed clothes before we got on the bus. We were definitely in the jungle now! Nobody really minded, however, since the landscape now looked exactly like what you would think a rain forest would look like – lush tropical trees, ferns and plants all along the river banks without any signs of civilization anywhere as we paddled downstream. Juan told us to keep an eye out for wildlife, as there would be many snakes, birds and lizards for the sharp-eyed tourist to spot. This was the jungle experience we had signed on for!

The four days we spent in the rain forest camp were exactly what they hoped they would be. The huts we were in had no electricity, but they did have flush toilets and beds with mosquito netting. In the morning you had to check your shoes to make sure there wasn't some type of bug, lizard or snake curled up inside before you stuck your foot in. We also got to see a few tarantula spiders crawling on the sides and roofs of the thatched huts, which really wasn't as creepy as it sounds.

We even took a few nighttime expeditions to search for caimans (aka *crocodiles*) in the water, and thanks to Juan's eagle eyes, we found a few, floating just below the surface with just their eyes and the very tops of their heads poking out of the water. As long as we had a flashlight shining in their eyes they didn't make a move, but swam quickly away from us once the light was gone. Kind of spooky, but also exciting at the same time.

One afternoon, Juan took us out in the canoe to fish for piranha. He gave each of us a length of fishing line with a hook and a small ball of hamburger to bait it with. Everyone dropped their lines over the side, and sure enough, within minutes one of the girls in the group caught one! Juan carefully pulled it off the hook and threw it back into the river. A few minutes later someone else caught one and the procedure was repeated. Yo even caught one without much trouble, but I couldn't seem to pull one in before it ate all my hamburger bait.

After the piranha fishing expedition, Juan suggested we try swimming in the river. This seemed a little strange to me since we had just seen how well stocked the river was with piranha fish, and we had already seen several crocodiles during our night time excursions. However, Juan assured us that with the splashing and rapid motions we would make with our arms and legs while swimming that we would scare any piranhas and crocs away. Then he jumped over the side of the canoe to prove he was telling the truth.

At first I wasn't sure I wanted to try this, even if it was totally safe, as Juan claimed. But then, each one of the twenty something males in the group dove over the side, and I decided I couldn't be the only man who wouldn't swim in the river with crocs and piranhas, so I jumped in with them. Needless to say, since I'm still here to tell the story, Juan was right. After all the men had gone in, a few of the females jumped in too, but there were still a few that just didn't want to get wet, so they stayed in the canoe.

All of our excursions were pretty interesting, including an early morning trip to a cluster of trees with around a *hundred* spider monkeys perched in the upper branches. We all rose at about 6:00 am, as instructed the night before and paddled the canoe between the trunks of the trees sticking out of the water. Then we just sat and watched the monkeys jumping from branch to branch just a few feet over our heads. It was truly an awesome sight and we made sure we got some great pictures to memorialize this adventure. My favorite image was when a few of the monkeys would jump from one tree to another over our heads and then turn around and stare down at us with a puzzled look on their faces. It seemed like if they could talk they might have said, "I sure wouldn't get up at 6:00 a.m. to come look at *you*! Don't you have anything better to do?"

The one expedition that I did find a little disturbing was a night time expedition to find exotic jungle insects. We all piled into the canoe and Juan guided us out to an island in the middle of the river which was supposed to have a good variety of spiders and bugs. He told us not to worry about any of the insects, no matter how big they were, because they were all virtually harmless. But then he said something that made we wonder for the first time, how wise it was to be wandering around in the Amazon rain forest at night.

"The only thing you have to be careful about is the poisonous snakes here," he said. "You probably won't be able to see them because they blend in with the ground and they have the same colors as the leaves, but don't step on them, because if they bite you, you could die in about a couple of hours."

Then he walked on, leading the way with his flashlight.

From that moment until we returned to the canoe to go back to the hut, I kept my flashlight trained on the ground in front of my feet and walked *very* carefully through the jungle island. Juan found some ungodly big crickets and other insects and even let them crawl on his face while the rest of the group took pictures of him, but I for one, didn't care about how many tricks he could do with jungle bugs. All I wanted to do was keep an eye on the ground until we were off that bloody island.

After our four days in the rain forest were finished we continued on to visit Isla de la Plata, an off shore island, which is sometimes known by the nickname of "The Poor Man's Galapagos" because of the rare birds, seals and lizards that live there. We went ashore to see some of these rare island birds called the Blue Footed Booby in it's natural habitat!

These were pretty large birds, about the size of a large goose, and they really, truly did have blue feet! Since they were an endangered species, it was illegal to touch them or try to harm them in any way, so if you came across one standing on the trail you had to carefully walk around it. Since they were so well protected, they had lost all fear of humans and would stand in the middle of the path, openly defying you to get close to them. We found out later, though, that the males usually do this only when they feel they have to protect their mates or offspring in a nearby nest. Since we didn't want to cause any problems with their family lives, we simply took pictures of the Boobies and left them alone.

On the boat coming back from the island, we got an extra special bonus – we encountered a pod of about 7 or 8 whales that swam alongside us for almost an hour. Their heads and dorsal fins broke through the surface every 4 or 5 minutes, which gave us a chance to take some awesome pictures, but they dove back down as quickly as they appeared, so it was almost impossible to get a good shot of them. Still the experience alone was awesome enough!

Everything went fine in Ecuador....until we stopped at a local internet café to make reservations for the next step of our journey. We had used internet cafes throughout our trip to find a reasonable place to stay each night for the next leg of our journey. We were in the middle of doing the same thing in Ecuador when we got into a mini argument about where we wanted to make a reservation for the next night, and I simply walked out to the street in my annoyance. Yo was a little annoyed with me too (hard to believe, I know). Unfortunately, one of the by-products of our annoyance was that neither one of us remembered that the backpack with our two cameras in it was sitting on the floor next to the desk we were using to find a room on the internet.

We did remember about a half hour later and made a mad dash back to the café. There we learned how important it is to observe the first rule of traveling – anywhere: always keep an eye on your belongings! The backpack was gone, and with it, our cameras and all the pictures we took in the rainforest and our trip to Isla de la Plata! The rain forest huts, the spider monkeys in the trees, the huge jungle insects, the Blue Footed boobies – all gone. Now we would have to rely strictly on our memories of these strange, wonderful sights.

It was a hard pill to swallow, but it also taught us a very important lesson. No matter where you go in the world, remember: one man's holiday trip is another man's opportunity to acquire new *stuff*!

$\mathscr{P}atagonia$

"Two drifters, off to see the world
There's such a lot of world to see"

-Johnny Mercer
Moon River

The trips to San Pedro de Atacama, Peru and Ecuador were all fantastic, but we waited until the school year for the international school was over for the best one of all: Patagonia. The school year in Chile ends right before Christmas, which seems a little strange until you realize that it's below the equator, which means that the seasons there are the exact opposite of the seasons above the equator. So the end of the school year and the beginning of summer in Chile happens right before Christmas. I finished teaching my last ESL class at the Universidad de Catolica del Norte on December 22nd, and we were on a plane on our way to Punta Arenas on the afternoon of the 23rd.

We actually arrived in Punta Arenas on Christmas Eve, December 24th. This was the place some people referred to as "the end of the world", simply because it was almost, but not quite, the southernmost tip of Chile. That would actually be Cape Horn, the infamous point where many sailing ships ended up on the rocks in the 1700s and 1800s, but that was about 50 miles further southeast. But anyway, this was the most southernmost city in Chile and also a jumping off point for cruise ships to Antarctica, so we felt the title was pretty appropriate.

It was pretty quiet when we got there – most businesses and public buildings were already closed or closing for Christmas, and even though it was the beginning of summer, south of the equator, the weather was on the wet and windy side. Hey, they don't call it the end of the world for nothing! But all in all, we spent a pretty quiet two days there, exploring the parks and hillsides in town, taking a few pictures and enjoying a nice Christmas dinner at one of the seaside hotels. The big excitement would take place the day after Christmas, when we shipped out to Magdalena Island.

Magdalena Island is a famous penguin reserve located about 40 minutes north of Punta Arenas in the Straits of Magellan. We bundled up to fend off the cold breezes off the water and boarded a tour boat with 50 or 60 other tourists a little after noon. Although the wind was steady, it wasn't freezing, thanks to the fact that we were there in early summer. When we finally reached the island and the boarding ramp was lowered, we looked out onto this small, bare, rocky island and saw some of the 120,000 Magellanic penguins that populate it. There were several rows of them, grouped in bunches of 3 or 4, up to 6 or 7 together, which made it look like there were several welcoming committees waiting to greet us when we came ashore.

The whole effect of the scenery was completely surreal. There were no buildings or structures on the island except for a small, ancient lighthouse at the very top of the highest hill on the island. We were told we only had an hour to spend there, so all the tourists naturally began walking up the roped off path up to the lighthouse where you could get the best panoramic picture views. On either side of the path, and all over the island were hundreds of burrows approximately 2 or 3 feet deep where penguin couples lived and, and on the day we were there, quite a few young chicks. The chicks were distinguishable from the adults by their fuzzy gray feathers, compared to the stark black and white coloring of their parents.

Everywhere you looked, the penguins were either strolling casually along and across the path, in between the burrows, along the rocky beach and anywhere else they pleased. Since they were all on a protected reserve, they could get away with ignoring the humans who ventured on their island, and they did. Everyone had been told beforehand that you couldn't even touch one of them without incurring an extremely onerous fine.

That was fine with us, and everyone else on the tour, as far as we could tell. All anybody wanted was to be able to take plenty of pictures to amaze their friends back home with, and that's exactly what we did. It certainly wasn't exciting in the sense of there being any danger involved, but it was so strange to be able to get close to literally hundreds of penguins during the short time we were there that it was definitely an unforgettable experience.

Our next stop was a town further up the coast called Puerto Natale, which was a few miles away from an incredible national park called Torres del Paine. While we were there we took a guided tour to see the wonders of this place, and they were definitely wonderous. The landscape consisted of rugged, snow-capped mountains, pristine glacier lakes and a few genuine glaciers as well. We had a beautiful day to enjoy some jaw-dropping scenery and take some great pictures. The main reason for coming to Puerto Natales, however, was because we would be taking a cruise on a cargo/passenger ship through the straits and fjords that abounded between there and our ultimate destination of Puerto Montt.

The "cruise ship" we took was actually a ferry that took 3 and ½ days to travel through the fjords and channels, which was the perfect itinerary for us on our journey up the coast. The date of our departure was actually on New Year's Eve, and it turned out to be a night to remember.

We weren't able to board the ship until around 8:00 pm that evening, and being two of the few passengers arriving without a car, we stood outside the gates to the road which led to the auto ramp until almost all of the cars boarding the ship had passed. Since this was the beginning of summer south of the equator, and because we were so far south, there was still plenty of daylight left as we boarded, as the sun didn't set until well after 9:00 pm. We took a quick look around the ship until we were able to find out where our cabin was and went there to unload our luggage.

When we go to our four-person cabin, we met our roommates—a Frenchwoman in her late thirties and her mother! I never imagined sharing a cabin on a ship with three women, so this was something of a surprise, although not an unpleasant one. They both spoke very good English, so we were able to converse easily. They also seemed very pleasant and easy to get along with, so we stored our suitcases and backpacks into the lockers inside the cabin and went up to the top deck for the "welcome aboard" party.

Because this was a ferry and not a cruise ship, the party room in the observation deck was just barely big enough to accommodate the 60 or 70 passengers crowded into it. I'm sure this particular ferry always had "welcome aboard" parties for the first day or night that new passengers came on board, but this was also New Year's Eve, so everyone was particularly eager to celebrate. Even though Yolande and I didn't speak much Spanish, we were able to enjoy some of the free champagne and snack food the ship's stewards brought out a few minutes before midnight and I did my best imitation of a semi-coordinated dance while the ship's sound system played some of the more popular Chilean dance music of the day.

After we got our champagne and a plateful of goodies, we looked for a place to sit. Most of the passengers seemed to be divided up into family units of four people or more, and most of them had been camped out in the available seats and lounge chairs for some time beforehand. It looked like the only place we could get a seat was at one of the three empty stools in front of the ship's tiny bar.

I walked over to one of the empty stools, and just before I got there a young couple took two of the remaining seats. Now there was only one left in the entire room, and I could see a tall, stout, older man with dark eyebrows and grey hair eyeing the same seat I was heading towards. I managed to get to the last remaining stool about two steps ahead of him and planted myself on it.

The man looked a little bit annoyed, but I thought "Hey, my ass is just as deserving as yours", and didn't think much more about it. Yolande came over to stand next to me while she finished her drink and hors d'oeuvres. I offered her my hard-earned seat, but she was content to stand.

About this time, the young couple seated next to me introduced themselves and the woman admitted she was an American, just like me (a bit of a rarity in this part of the world), and her husband was a native Chilean who was studying at Georgetown in Washington, D.C. Not only were they very friendly towards us, they also asked us if we wanted to join them in an extra bottle of champagne that they had brought on board. It didn't take an awful lot of persuasion and pretty soon we were downing a few more glasses of the bubbly.

After the champagne was gone, we all broke down and started buying drinks from the ship's bartender. At some point one of the other passengers finally vacated one of the other barstools and the tall, stout man that I had to race for my seat reappeared. He sat down on the stool next to me and said hello. I returned his greeting and then he told me his name was Alistair. He was a retired veterinarian from England and after we started talking he didn't seem like such a bad guy. We said "Happy New Year", toasted each other, and before long we were definitely in a friendlier mood. The young couple moved out onto the dance floor while Alistair and I decided to guard the bar and keep the bartender busy.

A few minutes later, Renee, the French woman who was one of our cabin mates appeared and Alistair began buying drinks for her and doing his best to get to know her better. Yolande decided it was time to go to bed, but I was in the mood to continue to drink in the New Year. It had been quite a few years since I had celebrated New Year's Eve, and now that I was in a party mood amongst some people with a similar disposition, I didn't want it to end too early. However, after another 30 minutes or so, it became obvious that all of Alistair's conversation from that point on would be directed towards Renee, so I decided I would call it a night too.

I found my way below decks to the maze of passageways that led to the cabins and somehow even found the right cabin. I opened the door and carefully made my way to the lower bunk on our side of the cabin in total darkness. Renee's mother had already drawn the curtain over her bunk on the opposite side and from the faint glimmer of light coming through the porthole, I could just make out Yolande lying in the top bunk on our side.

I was doing my best to be quiet and gracefully slide into the lower bunk, when suddenly either the boat rocked, or I finally felt the effects of three hours of drinking, and I fell flat on my face onto the floor. I didn't hear any sound from the other side of the cabin, but I could definitely hear Yo laughing. She was obviously still awake and had witnessed the whole performance. She asked if I was alright. I think I said yes, but within seconds I had plopped down into the bottom bunk and passed out cold. Happy New Year!

Around 7:30 that morning, I woke up with the painful knowledge that I had to find a bathroom fast. I then realized that during our boarding onto the ship and all during our New Year's Eve celebrations a few hours before, that I had neglected to find out where the bathrooms were (again, this wasn't a real "cruise ship", which meant that the bathrooms were not in the cabins). I quickly pulled on my pants and ran out of the cabin, searching for the nearest toilet in a T shirt and bare feet.

I reasoned that because I hadn't seen any bathrooms inside the passageways to the cabins that they must be on the outside somewhere. I ran out onto the deck and noticed the ship had left the dock and was now sailing speedily through the icy waters. I also realized three other rather important facts: I was the only person out on the deck that early, it was raining ice cold raindrops on me, and my bare feet were standing on what felt like frozen steel!

Needless to say, this made my search even more urgent and I desperately started running up and down the deck, looking frantically for a bathroom. I was getting so panicked that I was starting to ponder the consequences of just dropping my pants and aiming over the side of the ship. Suddenly, I saw one of the ship's crew walking on the other end of the deck in a bright orange raincoat and rain pants. I started running towards him and yelled out one of the few Spanish phrases I knew: *"Senor! Donde estal banos? Por favor!"*

The crewman saw me running in place in my bare feet in the rain and couldn't help but laugh. He waved me towards him and walked back into one of the passageways. I followed him at a trot as he led me through the maze inside the ship. After a couple of minutes which seemed more like eternity he stopped and pointed to a door on the side of one of the passageways. I did notice that the door had "Hombres" written on it in big letters and mumbled "Gracias!" as I rushed through the door.

A few minutes later my emergency was solved and I walked out of the bathroom door trying to figure out how to get back to my cabin. I didn't have to think very long, though. I looked at the numbers on the cabin doors along the hallway and came to the stunning conclusion that my cabin was directly in front of me, about 10 feet from the bathroom door! Obviously when I ran out the door five minutes earlier, my physical and mental state were in such a traumatic state that I never even saw it.

I was extremely grateful that I found that crewman when I did, and even more grateful that I remembered how to say *"Donde estal banos???"*

****

The rest of our trip through Patagonia was pretty much uneventful. Beautiful and enjoyable, but not eventful. We continued on our voyage through the fjords and islands off the coast until we reached Puerto Montt. We disembarked along with the rest of the passengers and spent a couple of hours exploring the town and taking pictures with two other couples that we had met on board the ship. From there we traveled to the island of Chiloe along with Alistair, the stout Englishman that we met at the "welcome aboard" party on New Year's Eve and later become good friends with.

He convinced us to stay at a rural "agri-tourism" hotel on the island which was run by a Chilean farming family consisting of an elderly couple and two sons and their wives who all worked together to provide lodging and meals in a large 7 or 8 bedroom farmhouse. Alistair warned us that it was not a typical tourist attraction, but instead was an opportunity to relax and experience the peacefulness and beauty of the Chilean countryside for 3 days.

We took him up on his offer, and discovered he was right about this being a welcome change of pace on our journey. The farmhouse we stayed in was located at the top of a hill which overlooked a valley with rolling fields of various types of vegetable crops, along with several pastures with cows, sheep and goats in residence. The island was situated in an area of Chile with mild year round temperatures, similar to central and northern California, which was perfect for the many crops which were grown there. The landscape, however looked exactly like Ireland to me with its green rolling hills and valleys. Although it was true there wasn't a lot to do there, as Alistair had told us, especially during the one day of solid rain, the scenery and the food that was included more than made up for it.

The mother of the clan was the official cook for the farmhouse and she spent the entire cooking incredible meals for us. The food was so delicious and we ate so much of it that we definitely needed to take a few hikes to walk some of the extra calories off. We did take one short bus trip to see the main town on the island and look for some scenic places for pictures, but other than that, we just spent 3 lazy days enjoying the countryside, just as Alistair recommended.

After Chiloe we continued up the coast by bus to visit Pucon, which was an interesting tourist town with a slightly active volcano. We had an opportunity to climb to the top of the volcano, but were warned that it was a pretty strenuous climb that took a minimum of 6 hours to get to the top and enjoy the privilege of looking into the crater. Since we felt that we had already seen enough volcanoes up close in Hawaii, we decided to pass. Instead we visited a national park nearby which required a 3 hour hike up the side of a mountain to see and take pictures of a beautiful alpine lake at the top. The temperature was in the upper 80s and this, combined with the effort required to hike up the steep trail on a hot, muggy day was plenty of exercise in my book, so we were glad we passed on the volcano!

We continued by bus up the coast, staying at hostels and/or cheap motels along the way and visited the cities of Valparaiso, Vina del Mar and Valdivia before ending up in Santiago for our flight back to Antofagasta. Each one of these stops had significant points of interest and were definitely worthwhile. Valparaiso had the biggest collection of colorful homes and cottages nestled alongside the nine hulls that surround the city that I had ever seen. The photo opportunities were many, and we took advantage of them. Vina del Mar was an interesting little beach town that looked very similar to many similar towns in southern California. Valdivia was a colonial seaport which featured a re-enactment of the battle of independence between the Spanish and Chilean armies in 1820. Even though the soldiers on both sides of the battle were clearly teen agers, it was still fun to watch the Chileans drive out the Spanish army, once and for all. By the time we got to Santiago, the only thing left to do was get to the airport to take our flight back to Antofagasta.

Chile was definitely a great experience. We had a few ups and downs, of course, but overall it was an incredible journey. Like all good things, however, it did have to come to an end at some point. Since our earnings from teaching were not exactly on the exorbitant side, by the time we had finished with our trip from Punta Arenas northward, we definitely needed to replenish our cash reserve. We decided the best way to do this was for me to return to California in early February to work on a short term project I had been offered by my former employer, and for Yo to meet me there within a few weeks.

Yo decided to stay behind to give the international school enough notice to allow them to find a replacement teacher before she left. Ordinarily, the teachers hired by the school were supposed to stay there for two years, but our contract agreements had been breached in so many ways that we didn't feel a bit guilty in telling them that Yo would be leaving Chile to re-join me in the U.S. within a matter of weeks. Of course, the school wasn't happy about it, but we weren't very happy with the broken promises we had to endure during out time there either. So, all in all, we figured it all evened out in the end. I booked my flight back to the U.S. and went back to Antofagasta to get ready for my return.

We had lots of great experiences in Chile. The trips to San Pedro de Atacama, Peru, Ecuador and the Patagonia were once-in-a-lifetime, amazingly scenic trips. There were other interesting episodes as well, not all of them fun, but definitely memorable.

One of the main lessons we both had to learn was that the Chileans love parties and music, and they don't care if anyone else wants to hear it, once they start to party, they don't stop until dawn – literally. The first time I realized this was during our first month at the international school. It was during the time that I had torn my hamstring and was laid up in our apartment for two and a half weeks. On the first or second Friday we were there and classes were in full swing, one of the apartments directly above ours had a party and the hosts and the guests were singing, laughing and talking with all the windows open and also out on the balcony for their unit. Normally, things like that don't bother me, but this time I started seething when it got to be around 2:00 or 3:00 am. , and there didn't seem to be any sign that the noise was going to stop anytime soon. It probably didn't help my mood any that I was still in a lot of pain from the torn hamstring and desperately needed to get some sleep. I poked my head out of our window a few times to see who in the world these people were that had no respect for anyone else, and kept partying, very loudly, well into the wee hours of the morning.

I could see several people sitting out on the balconies a floor or two above us, seemingly oblivious as to how loud they were at such a late hour, and I temporarily lost control of my temper.

"SHUT UP!" I yelled, as loud as possible, and then quickly ducked my head back into our apartment.

The music and the laughing stopped, and you could hear a pin drop for maybe 30 seconds. Then the noise returned, as loud as ever, so obviously nobody cared whether anyone else was annoyed with the partying.

The celebration went on all night, until around 7:00 a.m., when the sun started to rise, we could finally hear people leaving and walking out into the street through the main entrance directly two floors below us. I decided I wanted to get a look at some of the people leaving to see just what kind of inconsiderate morons thought that it was alright to disturb someone else's sleep all night long, regardless of what they were celebrating.

I limped out of bed, and slowly made my way to the sliding glass door that led out onto our balcony to get a look at some of the despicable partiers. I tried to stay just behind the curtain, out of sight of anyone who happened to look up to see me watching them.

Unfortunately, a young man leaving with two female friends happened to look up while I was looking down and spotted me. He immediately started laughing, as I tried to back away, but then, since I knew I was spotted anyway, decided to stand there and stare at them.

Not only were they not intimidated, they started laughing mockingly at me and all three of them gave me the middle finger salute. Part of me wanted to jump over the balcony to the ground two floors below, but fortunately, my brain was still working well enough to realize that I would probably break my leg in doing so, which would be really stupid, so I managed to control the impulse. In addition, I wasn't sure what the backgrounds of the people at the party were and thought I might be asking for trouble from the less law abiding segments of the Antofagasta citizenry if I decided to confront these three, torn hamstring and all. It amazes me now to think that I actually considered doing this, but at the time I was working very hard to control my anger and the abundance of stupidity that it usually triggered. I finally realized that it wasn't anything worth fighting about anyway, and I probably did look pretty stupid trying to hide behind the curtains to watch the party-goers leave, so after a minute or two I gave them a "what the hell" smile and waved goodbye. Of course, this made them even more exultant and defiant, so they yelled and gave me the finger even more, but by that time I was too tired to do anything about it and decided to just go back to bed and try to get a few minutes' sleep.

This was only the first of many sleepless weekends, at least as far as Friday and Saturday nights were concerned, and we soon learned that this was really the norm in Chile. You either had to find a party to go to on the weekends, or you learned to live without sleep for a couple of nights. We did get a few opportunities to join the other teachers in a few "all night" parties ourselves, but being the elder statesmen of the group, we were usually gone long before the sun came up, so we never became fully *"naturalized"* Chileans.

After I stopped teaching at the international school, Yo and I had to find another apartment because the one the school provided was for teachers only, and if I wasn't teaching there I could not receive this benefit. So we found another two person apartment a short bus ride away from the school which was brand new, fully furnished with all appliances and a big screen TV, and best of all it was located on the 21st floor, high above the noise and celebrations that usually took place every weekend – or so we thought. We found out that even being that high up could not protect us from the Chilean party habits.

I returned to the apartment very late one evening from working at the mine on one of my weekly two day trips. I was surprised to hear some very loud music coming from the apartment door at the end of our hallway. Since Yo had to teach the next day at the international school, she was already in bed by the time I arrived at my customary time around 10:30 pm. I came inside our apartment and watched TV or checked my email messages for a few minutes before trying to go to bed around 11:00 p.m.

I assumed that since it was a Wednesday night, there couldn't be any type of national holiday being celebrated, so maybe it was a birthday party or something along those lines. As such, I figured it would have to break up soon because most people in the building probably had to go to work the next day. As the minutes wore on, and the music from a stereo system inside the apartment continued to blast away, I became more and more annoyed. Once again I tried to wait as long as I possible could before resorting to a direct confrontation, but when the music didn't subside after 11:30, I decided it was time, once again, to take a stand.

I had never met any of the people in the apartment at the end of the hall. Indeed, we had never met any of the other tenants period. We all basically came and went in our high rise anonymity without ever speaking to each other except once in a while on the elevator. Therefore, I didn't know what to expect after I knocked loudly on the door.

At first there was no answer, so I knocked again, even louder. This time there were one or two voices shouting something above the music and the volume suddenly went down a few notches. Still, no one had answered the door, so I knocked again, just as loud as the last time. I hear the sound f feet shuffling back and forth inside and the volume decreased somewhat again. As I heard the door handle start to turn from the inside, I expected to see a semi-sober teen ager or young adult on the other side of the door, and prepared for what I thought could be a defiant encounter.

To my surprise, when the door opened I was suddenly fact to face with an elderly Chilean man, probably in his mid to late seventies. Far from being defiant or hostile, he seemed almost pleased that I was there. I assumed he didn't speak much English, but since I probably spoke even less Spanish, I just told him in English "Could you please turn the music DOWN?"

He seemed a little puzzled at this, so I said again "The MUSIC! Can you turn the music DOWN?" I said, pointing to my ears. This time he got it.

"Oh, si! Si!" he said and smilingly closed the door. Within a few seconds the volume of the music went down considerable and I walked back to our apartment. A few minutes later, I got into bed and heard the music stop completely and heard footsteps in the hallway. I jumped out of bed to go look through the peephole in our door and saw two or three adult women saying goodbye and walking towards the elevator. I got the impression that this might have been a birthday party for the old man and perhaps the women were his daughters helping him celebrate.

I felt a little guilty for breaking up their party, but then, it *was* Wednesday night, and Yo *did* have to get up early for her class, so I felt I was justified. At least I didn't have to deal with a half drunk Chilean giving me the finger this time. So we were able to end the confrontation peacefully, but it also reinforced the lesson that Chileans loved to party and for them, the music was never too loud, no matter what time of the night or what day of the week. As everyone always told us, you have to be "flexible" to work in Chile. Either that or be deaf or able to live without sleep!

****

Back To The Future

"All God's children get weary when they roam
Don't it make you want to go home?
Now tell me, don't it make you want to go
home?"

-Joe South
Don't It Make You Want to Go Home?

When it came time to finally leave Chile, it was definitely more difficult than I thought it would be. When I first arrived there, I was working for the international school and they were supposed to take care of all the legalities related to obtaining and paying for our work visas. They usually took care of the tourist visas that you needed just to come to Chile, but then it seemed like their commitment to taking care of the business visa requirements which were needed to continue to live and work there were very inconsistent. Many of the teachers there waited for almost two years before they were finally able to get their "permanent" visas, and some of them never actually got them until they were almost done with their two year assignments.

We never really understood how some of the teachers were able to get their visas within a month or two after arriving, while others had to continuously make the trip to El Centro (aka "downtown") to the visa and immigration offices to get an extension on their temporary visas. After I stopped working at the international school and started teaching with the King's Language Institute, I had to make a couple of trips to the visa office, and each time I was able to take a fellow teacher who was bi-lingual to guide me through the process. In the meantime, once I stopped teaching at the end of December and went on the three week tour of Patagonia and southern Chile, I didn't even think about any visa issues, since I knew I would be leaving the country within a few weeks.

Since Yolande chose to stay for at least the first month of the new school year, I would be leaving on my own at the end of January and she planned to re-join me in California by early March. I didn't particularly want to be separated from her for over a month, but I had a project job assignment waiting for me to start working on in February, so for practical reasons, that was the best way to do it. So on the last day of January I kissed Yo goodbye, called a taxi and headed to the airport for the first leg of my return to America.

The process of checking my baggage and going through security all went very smoothly without any problems. Then I got to the customs checkpoint. I walked up to the glass booth with a man sitting inside wearing a suit and tie and passed my passport and visa paperwork to him under the space provided at the bottom of the window. He looked at my passport picture, punched something into his keyboard and looked at his monitor. A slightly puzzled look came over him and he looked at my passport and visa again and punched in some more numbers on his keyboard. Finally, after a few minutes he looked at me and passed my passport and visa document back to me and said "No."

I looked at him and tried to figure out what was wrong. He shook his head and again looked at me and said "No." I gave him the international sign for "WTF" by standing in front of him and raising my open palms to the sky. He reeled off something in Spanish that I couldn't understand. The security guard who was standing by and witnessing the entire process stepped up to me and said "You cannot board the plane. Your visa has expired."

I looked at him and said "It doesn't matter. I'm leaving the country."

"Yes, senor, I know. But you have to get your visa renewed."

"No," I told him. "You don't understand. I'm not coming into Chile. I'm leaving. I'm LEAVING to go BACK to America!"

He shook his head again. "Yes, senor, I understand. But you must still get your visa renewed."

I couldn't believe what I was hearing. "You mean I have to get my visa renewed to LEAVE Chile?" I asked.

"Si, senor. You cannot leave until your visa is up to date."

I tried to tell him that I had already checked my bags and he said he would notify the baggage handlers that I had to get them back. I tried to tell him that it was ridiculous for me to need a visa to leave the country, and if they would just let me through, I promised I would never come back again.

No matter what I said it didn't matter. They weren't going to let me leave because my visa had expired about two weeks prior. I had remembered that it was expiring after the end of December, and I completely forgot about it after that, thinking I wouldn't need it beyond that date since I wouldn't be teaching in Chile any longer at that time. I never imagined that I would need to have a current visa to leave the place!

So I trekked back to the baggage counter, told the clerk my sad tale of woe and eventually got my luggage back. Then I took a taxi back to our apartment and told it Yolande, who was very surprised to see me back three within a few hours of leaving to return to the U.S.

I called Ariel, my bi-lingual friend and fellow teacher from the Kings Language Institute and begged him to accompany me to the lawyer's office who handled visa renewals in El Centro the next day. To my surprise he agreed to help me out, even though we no longer worked together and I probably wouldn't see him again. He didn't seem to mind. Like most Chileans we met, and actually like most South Americans we met, he was a very friendly person who usually tried to help you if he could.

So bright and early the next morning Ariel and I met outside the lawyer's office who handled visa issues for almost all of the foreign teachers in the city. We went in after he talked his way past the receptionist and took the elevator up to the third floor.

As soon as we got off the elevator we saw a long line of around 15 or 16 people waiting to see the very same lawyer we had to see, and we knew it would be a long day. The line moved at a snail's pace and around noon time we still had at least 6 or 7 people ahead of us. I had resigned myself to the fact that we would be there all day, but when the secretary came out to announce that the lawyer was taking his lunch break, Ariel said something to her in Spanish and she told him that if we came back after lunch, we would be the first ones in to see him!

We were both pretty hungry by this time, but I didn't want to take any chances on losing my place, so we just sat and waited. About 15 minutes later the secretary reappeared and miraculously called my name! I went into the lawyer's office with Ariel joining me as my interpreter.

The lawyer's desk was completely covered with documents piled up about a foot high in some places. He looked at my passport and visa documents, asked Ariel a few questions, which he answered and punched some data into his computer keyboard. Within minutes a new visa document emerged from his printer with spaces for new expiration dates. The lawyer told me in fairly good English, that the visa was being extended until February 12th, but I could not stay in Chile any longer than that under any circumstances. I assured him that I would be long gone by then and probably wouldn't ever be back. He seemed satisfied with this, so he filled in the dates on the renewal form and handed it back to me along with my passport.

"Good luck," he said.

"Muchas Gracias," I answered.

After that there wasn't much to do except to pay Ariel a few pesos for all the time he spent waiting with me and go back to my apartment to make new travel arrangements. Within a few days, I had set up a new itinerary and was ready to fly back to America.

This time they let me on the plane and the next night I was back in L.A., ready to start my contract job and replenish my critically low cash fund. I had to postpone a visit to my daughter in Hawaii as a result of the re-scheduling, but I was happy to be back on my native soil, no matter how crazy it might get at times. The experience in Chile was definitely beneficial overall. Yolande and I traveled to a lot of places and saw a lot of incredible sites we wouldn't be able to see otherwise, but it was till good to be home. As always, I learned some valuable lessons while I was there, but the one that I'll never forget was : Always keep your visa up to date when you're in a foreign country, even if the only thing you want to do there is **leave**!

****

Canada

"Clowns to the left of me
Jokers to the right,
Here I am
Stuck in the middle with you"

-Gerry Rafferty and Joe Egan
Stuck in the Middle With You

Coyote Lake (or a town with a name very much like that) is officially described as a hamlet in northern Alberta, Canada. In reality, however, it is the site of land reserved for a First Nations group, commonly called a "band", which for purposes of this book, we'll call the "Wild Hawk First Nation", but in many ways it is located on another planet.

According to Mapquest ®, the distance between Long Beach, California and Coyote Lake is a little more than 2,000 miles, which in theory could be driven in as little as two days. However, since there were 3 major national parks on the way there, we had no intention of rushing our journey, so we took a full 5 days to get there.

We had volunteered to work for the Wild Hawk First Nation band for 10 months in return for having our lodging and living expenses paid, and we decided it would be a great road trip to take in late summer. In retrospect, we were glad we took the time to enjoy the spectacular landscapes along the scenic route, since that was just about the only thing that went right on this trip.

After we had returned from Chile, Yo and I moved back to Long Beach, and by a complete stroke of luck, back into the very same apartment we had rented for the 5 years before we left for China. I was fortunate enough to find a decent paying job working for a law firm in downtown L.A. and Yo went back to modeling for the various art schools scattered throughout L.A. County. In a short time, we had restored a big chunk of our cash reserves and were once again enjoying a safe, secure, pleasant lifestyle in Southern California.

Within 6 months I was bored out of my mind. I had to find something else to do with my life.

Yo had always warned me that once you started exploring new countries and experiencing new customs that it would be hard to settle for a regular 9 to 5 routine again, and boy, she was right. Even though I was actually making very good money for the simple reports I was preparing for the law firm, I chafed at having to sit at a desk all day long with almost no interaction with any other employees besides my boss. After a little more than a year at the law firm, I found myself checking out the foreign English teacher want ads on the internet again. Then, one day, I saw it.

"Volunteers wanted to work for a charitable foundation devoted to improving the educational and economic lives of First Nations communities in Canada. Free room and board, health insurance and all living expenses paid for 10 month assignment. Submit CV and picture for further consideration."

Those weren't actually the exact words on the listing, but close enough.

At first I thought Yo would think I was crazy to even consider volunteering in a part of the world where the temperature gets down to 40 degrees below zero in winter. Besides, we had already begun the application process and been interviewed by a school in Costa Rica where one of our colleagues from the international school in Chile was already working. We figured that with our connection from Chile that the teaching assignments in Costa Rica were pretty much in the bag. However, eventually that opportunity fell through when the school accepted two other candidates for the position, so the possibility of volunteering in Canada began to sound better and better.

After a preliminary Skype interview with Winston, the CEO of the Economic Development group for the First Nation band in Coyote Lake, we were sold. We gave notice to our employers, terminated the lease on our apartment and sold all our furniture, just as we did before we moved to China 3 years earlier. Then we packed up our car to the point where both of us could barely see out of the back window and set off on another road trip, excited by the prospect of being able to teach and improve the educational and economic lives of a First Nations group in Canada!

Unfortunately, as Mick Jagger of the Rolling Stones once sang, *"You can't always get what you want!"* The assignment in Coyote Lake turned out to be the biggest disaster we experienced during all our travels.

We arrived at Coyote Lake after a five day journey through California, Oregon, Washington, British Columbia and Alberta. We stopped at Crater Lake National Park in Oregon and Banff and Jasper National Parks in Alberta. We saw some of the most beautiful scenery in North America. That was the fun part of our trip.

Once we drove onto the reservation the first problem we ran into was finding Winston.

Winston (not his real name) was the CEO for the Economic Development team for the "band" (aka "tribe") and he was an amazing, real-life success story. I had met him via a Skype interview after we had submitted our resumes and applications to the non-profit organization that we volunteered with.

He was extremely friendly, polite and impressive. I was fascinated to learn that he was a First Nations citizen himself who had been separated from his mother and sisters and relocated to one of the Canadian residential schools in the Northwest Territories as a young boy. He told me how the residential schools had been set up by the Canadian government as a means of "assimilating" aboriginal people into white Canadian culture (also sometimes called "killing the Indian" in aboriginal children). The treatment that he and the other native children received in these schools has to be one of the most shameful eras in North American history (although overall, confiscating the entire continent of North America from its indigenous people probably ranks first). From what Winston told me, life at the residential schools was more like being in a reformatory, or at best, similar to living in one of the internment camps used by the United States to round up Japanese Americans during World War Two. The environment within these schools was mostly harsh, dismal and hopeless, and many of the children placed in these "schools" ended up committing suicide as a result. In addition, the misery within the camps and schools sometimes caused people to become violent, which made life dangerous as well. Winston's mother was actually murdered in the camp she was sent to. Despite these hardships, Winston had lifted himself out of the depths of despair and became amazingly successful. He had degrees in business administration along with an MBA from the University of Alberta and had become a wealthy businessman who also worked with the non-profit organization.

I had two or three video Skype meetings with Winston during the months before we actually left for Canada and we had also exchanged several email messages. I knew that he was involved in many fund raising activities and meetings as part of his duties as the CEO for the economic development of the band. As a result, he often missed Skype meeting appointments or failed to respond to email messages for days at a time. This type of behavior worried me a little at first, but after talking with him a few times and learning about all the activities he was involved in, and hearing about the hardships he had overcome, I was convinced he could be trusted.

He had asked that we arrive in Coyote Lake by the last Wednesday in August in order to be there to meet some key contacts and enjoy the annual Treaty Days celebration which would begin that day and continue through the weekend. Because of some last minute snags in getting our working visas from the Canadian government, we had to leave California later than planned, but still managed to arrive late in the afternoon of the first day of Treaty Days.

Treaty Days was actually the celebration of the 25th anniversary of the signing of the Treaty Land Entitlement agreement between the Wild Hawk First Nation and the government of Canada. The flyer and schedule that Winston sent me sounded like it would be a terrific four day celebration complete with parades, live music, a traditional aboriginal village, pig races, a moose calling contest, a bounce house, games for kids and fireworks.

We weren't sure exactly what to expect in terms of road development and access to the reservation (which we couldn't even find on the Mapquest map) when we left our motel that morning in Edson, about 300 miles to the south. However, Winston had assured me that the roads to the "res" (aka *reservation*) would be accessible all year round, because Shell Oil was trucking out around 80,000 barrels of oil a day from its refinery about 15 miles away. Sure enough, the roads were remarkably well maintained for such a remote area, and we had no trouble following Winston's directions. We eventually rolled into the parking lot of the band office, just across from the school and fairgrounds late that afternoon.

In the large, grassy field next to the school we could see many tents set up with people sitting, talking, eating and sometimes dancing in the warm afternoon sun. There was a speaker system set up with a DJ blasting dance music out at a volume only teenagers could withstand. There was the advertised bounce house set up towards the rear of the property and there was even a roller hockey rink with two teams of kids battling it out on roller skates inside. In addition, there were several tents and tables set up selling a variety of snacks, traditional foods and soft drinks. Of course there were also lots of kids chasing each other and running all over the place. In short, it was a lot like a county fair or holiday weekend carnival, and everyone seemed to be having a good time.

We walked onto the field through an open section of chain link fencing and searched for some sign of the non-profit organization we had signed up with, or some sign of Winston himself. After a few minutes of walking along and through the various tents and booths without any luck, we tried to find the man whose voice kept making announcements through the loudspeakers next to a rectangular cement patio that had been converted into a temporary dance floor.

I spotted a young man who appeared to be the emcee for some type of contest that he was making announcements about. It took a little while to get his attention, as he was far more interested in teasing and joking with a group of teen age girls surrounding his makeshift microphone stand. When I finally did get him to hear me, I asked him if he could tell us how to find Winston.

"Who?" he asked.

"Winston. He's supposed to be the CEO for the Economic Development group for the Wild Hawk."(I assumed everybody in the reservation would know who this was.)

"Oh, I think I know who you mean," he said as he led me back out onto the field. He pointed at some distant body on the other side.

"I think that's him in the blue plaid shirt," he said. "I'm not really sure who he is, but I think I heard somebody tell me that Winston would be coming by in a little while and that he was the guy in the plaid shirt."

The young man then returned to the business of flirting with the girls around his microphone table. I looked across the field and started walking toward s the man in the blue plaid shirt. Somehow, he didn't look like the man I had spoken with in our Skype meetings. As I got a little closer, I knew it wasn't him.

Yolande and I were a little puzzled. Based on our telephone conversation with Winston just a couple of days before, he had assured us that he would be out on the fairgrounds during all of Treaty Days and he would be easy to find. "If you don't see me, just ask for me," he said. "Everybody knows me on the res."

Well, it seemed like perhaps not *everybody* knew him. We stopped at a spot that had been converted to a display of traditional First Nations teepees, with a burning campfire in front. Everyone seemed to be very busy doing something, and we felt a little guilty about stopping them, but we had to try to find Winston. We asked again.

This time the people we talked to seemed to know exactly who he was, but nobody seemed to know *where* he was. One of the Aboriginal people we asked said that Winston had been there a while ago, but didn't know where he was now. "He seems to have disappeared!"

"Yeah, he's good at that!" chimed in a large Aboriginal man sitting in a lawn chair near the campfire. He asked us why we were looking for him and when we told him we were the volunteers for the non-profit group he said "Oh, yeah, he told us you were coming. I thought he was going to be here to meet you?"

Yes, we told him, that's what we thought too. "Alright, well, why don't you just pull up a chair and sit down. We'll send somebody to find him", the large man told us.

We did as he suggested and made small talk with him and a few other Aboriginal people seated close by. The big man's name was Matthew, and although he didn't come out and say it, we could tell that he and Winston were probably not the best of friends. "I don't know why he didn't stay here to meet you", Matthew said. "But that's the way Winston does things. Ahh, don't worry, he'll be here eventually."

Finally, after about 30 or 40 minutes, Matthew was right. Winston did appear, and we gave each other the obligatory man hug and exchanged greetings. Winston started introducing Yolande and me to several people and told us how great it was that we could make it there for Treaty Days because there were lots of important people he wanted us to meet.

One of the important people we met turned out to be the Chief of the band. When Winston introduced us, I wasn't sure I heard him right because he didn't look like what I thought a Chief would look like. He was a tall, good looking man of about 35 or 36 with short dark hair, wearing a Native American vest of some sort and a friendly smile. On top of that, his name was Tyson, which didn't sound much like an Indian name to me.

"We had a little problem with your accommodations," Winston suddenly said to me. "We were supposed to have a separate cabin for you and Yolande, but there's been some problem getting it all set up. The band office was supposed to take care of it, but they didn't, and they're off now until after Treaty Days are over. But don't worry, you'll be able to stay at my house tonight," he said. "And then," he continued," either tomorrow night or the next night you'll move into Chief Tyson's house."

"Right!" Tyson said. "It's my house, but I don't live there. It's only about 40 minutes away in Peace River, but I like to stay here, on the reservation, so you can use it until we get one of the cabins set up for you."

Fine, I thought. I didn't really care where we slept that night as long as we didn't have to pay for another motel. And anyhow, if we just had to stay at Winston's house for a couple of nights, who cared? I was sure that it was a temporary problem that would get resolved as soon as the Treaty Days celebration was over. After all, we committed to coming there over two months earlier, so they knew we were coming and had to have made some kind of arrangements for us. Right?

Well, not quite. That night, we slept on an air mattress in one of the spare rooms in Winston's reservation house. We were part of a group of 6 other guests who were there for the Treaty Days celebrations. All of the other guests besides Yolande and I were First Nations people, including an elderly Chief from British Columbia who Winston told me was a descendent from Chief Seattle. (I never realized that the city of Seattle was named after a real person until then!) We sat in Winston's den for a few hours, struggling mightily to make conversation with the Chief and his two adult sons. It was somewhat difficult, given that we had no idea as to what their lifestyle was like, whether or not they lived on a reservation and most importantly, exactly what we would be doing there.

We knew I would be assisting Winston with writing grant requests and business plans, and that Yo would be assisting the teachers in the reservation school, but beyond that we were as clueless as everyone else. When the conversation came around to "So, what are *you* doing here?" that's exactly what we said. Even though it wasn't much of an explanation, it seemed to be good enough. After exhausting my small talk skills with the rest of the guests in Winston's den, Yo and I excused ourselves to go to bed in Winston's spare office room.

The next morning I had barely been awake for 10 minutes when my cell phone rang.

"Good morning, Michael. This is Winston. Sorry to call you so early, but we are having a meeting in the band office this morning with a major pipeline company to discuss the damages they owe to the band for an oil spill that happened two years ago." I was a little surprised that he would call me on my cell phone, when I was sleeping in his own house. However, I realized that he had probably already been up and was working at the band office." Would you like to sit in on it?"

Seeing as how my appointment book was totally blank for the day, I accepted the invitation. Thirty minutes later I met Winston at the band office about 200 yards from his house and joined him in a conference room inside.

The other people there included three other Caucasians and a First Nations man who identified themselves as representatives of the pipeline company. In addition, Matthew, the band member we met while searching for Winston the previous day was also there. I learned that Winston was the CEO for the Economic Development team, which meant he was involved in all the monetary and economic discussions and that Matthew was the environmental director for the band.

When I arrived at the band office to meet Winston prior to the meeting, he and Matthew were having an argument over something. Matthew said something like "Everyone at that table yesterday thought that you were rude!" to which Winston replied "We all agreed to it months ago!" Apparently, Matthew didn't recall the agreement and walked away muttering that that wasn't the way it happened. As we walked to the band office together, I asked Winston what it was all about.

"Ah, that's the way the people are here. They tell you one thing to your face and then they stab you in the back."

I asked him what he meant by this.

"He's complaining because he agreed months ago that you and your wife would be able to stay in his house. He gets a free house on the res because he's a band officer, but it's got four bedrooms and he's the only one in it. When I asked him if he could give you and Yolande a room to stay in two months ago he said 'Fine'! Then when I brought it up yesterday before you got here he said he never agreed to it. That's the kind of thing they do here! It drives me fucking crazy!"

I didn't quite understand then why this had become a problem, but in the days to come I would learn that Winston and Matthew had a huge dislike for each other and that each one resented the other one being an officer of the band. They both had big egos and had an ongoing power struggle that bubbled below the surface of all their meetings. In other words, the corporate world isn't the only place where politics is a significant part of daily business. In fact, in the coming weeks, I would learn that it was far more important in the First Nations world than anyplace else I had ever worked!

The first meeting with the pipeline company was relatively uneventful, except for two things: how slowly and formally the First Nations people moved in regard to running their meetings, and how big Matthew's ego was.

I learned that the issue of the valuation of the damages to be repaid to the band was complicated and controversial. The pipeline company had submitted a proposal which the band felt was extremely low, and most of the meeting consisted of Winston giving many examples of costs that the pipeline company had failed to consider, e.g. loss of hunting and trapping areas, the cultural suffering caused by the disturbance of sacred Aboriginal land, etc. Although the pipeline representatives seemed willing to entertain reparations for such costs, the method of determining their value was the biggest problem.

Winston was adamant that the geological expert the pipeline company had retained to assist with this task was incompetent for the assignment and Matthew agreed. Matthew also went on at length to inform everyone that he had been involved with a similar settlement with another pipeline company concerning another spill on a different band's land. It was obvious that he wanted the pipeline people to be impressed with his credentials, although it didn't appear that anyone could be as impressed as he was. I could see why Winston had indicated that he was a difficult person to work with.

I actually didn't have much to do at the meeting besides sit and listen. When it came my turn to announce to the group my title and why I was attending the meeting, I simply said "I don't know what my title is and I'm here to find out what I'm supposed to do!" This got a few laughs, but it was totally true. The sad part was that it would be true for most of my time at Coyote Lake.

After the meeting concluded, Winston and I went back out onto the fairgrounds to find Yolande. The Treaty Days celebration was still in full swing, and she was walking around the various booths and displays. We followed Winston around and after every 10 feet or so, he would introduce us to someone who was representing an oil company, or a pipeline company, or somebody who owned a trucking firm who wanted a contract to haul the waste from the nearby refinery, etc., etc., etc. Winston seemed like a consummate deal-maker, and it took the better part of an hour just to cross the fairgrounds due to all the people he wanted to introduce us to.

We spent the rest of the day wandering around and meeting various business contacts that Winston introduced us to. We also posed for pictures with Winston, Chief Tyson and several other First Nations people I don't remember. At the end of the day, we walked back to Winston's house for supper, and he told us what our first assignment as volunteers for the non-profit organization would be – to help him set up a stage in another town for a concert he had organized and was performing in the following night!

"A concert?" I asked.

"Yes! I have a concert arranged to benefit the school!" he said. "There's gonna' be three country bands and a comedian! I'm going to perform a song I wrote about my mother too! It's going to be a big fund raiser, and I'll need you and Yolande to help me get it all set up!"

OK, I thought. It seemed a little bit odd that I was just hearing about it the day before, but then I assumed that, since he was obviously an astute businessman and based on that morning's meeting, a meticulous planner, I thought it would be a great opportunity to learn something about concert promoting.

After dinner that night I met the comedian who would be performing at the concert. He turned out to be an old family friend who had just arrived in town and would *also* be staying at Winston's house that night. The good news was that the elderly

Chief and his two sons were leaving, so it wouldn't be quite as crowded as the night before, but Yo and I still slept in Winston's office that night. The next night, Winston informed me, we would be moving to Chief Tyson's house outside of Peace River.

The next day me, Yolande, Winston, the comedian and 4 others headed out in a three vehicle convoy to the town where the concert would be held, which was about 40 miles away. We drove to a two-story multi-purpose facility which included a hockey arena, a health club, a gymnasium, a space for art exhibits, a snack bar and a kitchen. My job, along with 2 other helpers, was to load up the plastic chairs which were to be used for the concert audienc and roll them through the complex to the hockey arena floor. The facilities manager told us there was a limit of 300 seats that could be placed in the arena. Then he asked Winston how many chairs he needed for the concert.

"Three hundred", he said.

Wow! I was impressed! This was going to be something! I didn't realize the groups Winston had booked for this gig could sell that many seats when the tickets cost $25.00 each, but then I didn't know who was performing either. I and two of the other guests from Winston's house hauled 300 chairs from a storage room to the arena floor on rolling carts. It took us about 3 hours altogether to get everything arranged and set to Winston's satisfaction. When we had finished, Yo and I got back into our car and the comedian and two of the others got into theirs and we all followed Winston to Tyson's house in Peace River about 10 miles away. The reason the others were joining us was because Winston had booked the arena and the bands playing there for not one night but two! So the comedian and two other band members would be staying at the house with us that night, so we could all return to the arena for the second concert the next night to take everything down.

We followed the van Winston was in to Peace River and turned off one of the main exits to a winding gravel round. The road led up the side of a very high hill called Kauffman's Mountain. I did my best to follow the van but there were so many curves in the road that at times, all I could see was the cloud of dust trailing behind it. When we finally got close to the summit, the van pulled into a long driveway.

We all pulled in and got out of our cars to see a huge 4 bedroom house with a surrounding deck and a separate horse barn and shed. As impressive as the house was, however, it could not compete with the view.

The house was built on top of a plateau with a view of the town of Peace River and the body of water with the same name about three fourths of a mile below. The view was absolutely breathtaking, and when the leaves changed color in the Fall it was a scene worthy of National Geographic. Winston told us we had to be back at the arena in about 5 hours, so we could take a look around town and get something to eat before we came back to take tickets and help with crowd control during the concert.

We all chose one of the bedrooms on the lower level, dropped off our backpacks and went upstairs to look around and enjoy the view. The other people staying in the house that night were the comedian and another elderly Chief and his female cousin, Dora. Apparently, the Chief had some medical problems and needed Dora to accompany him wherever he went. They both slept in separate bedrooms, so as far as I could tell, it was a true story.

There really wasn't much to do at the house once we unpacked. We had electricity, but no television, no phone and no internet. On top of that there wasn't much food left in the fridge, so Yolande and I decided we would take a tour of the town and get some lunch. Dora asked if she could join us, since the comedian and the Chief both wanted to take a nap, so we said why not. We decided we would stop in town for a little while, get something to eat and then continue on to the arena for our pre-concert duties. The Chief and the comedian would join us at the arena in the chief's car later.

When we got to the arena, Winston was already setting up a dressing room for the performers. He had me set up a table near the front entrance and Dora and I sat there ready to take tickets and handle the cash for any walk-in sales. A few of the band members walked in, some of them wearing cowboy hats, and all of them carrying guitar cases and other equipment. One by one, they gave us a quick look and a nod and walked back toward the hockey arena.

Meanwhile, Yolande was busy painting Winston's face in the authentic colors and symbols of a traditional First Nations ceremonial mask. Winston asked her to do this so that he could perform his original song about his mother, and the Aboriginal culture in traditional tribal colors.

The concert was advertised to begin at 8:00 p.m., with the doors opening at 7:30. Dora and I sat at our table with extra tickets to sell and money to make change before 7:15. Everything was in place to get the concert up and running and raise some money for the reservation school.

There was just one problem. *Nobody showed up! Not one warm body! Nobody! Nada! Zilch!*

Although I had assumed Winston was a good businessman and an experienced planner, based on his background, it appeared that marketing was not one of his strengths. He had given many books of tickets to the local radio stations and had them advertise the concert on their programs, but never checked back with them to see how many tickets had been given away. Even if he had, there was no guarantee that the tickets, which had been prizes for some of the stations' contests would ever be used. Apparently he had overestimated the demand for people in a rural area to come to a concert featuring little known acts at a price of $25.00 per person, even if it was for a worthy cause.

As my watch ticked past 7:30, then 7:45 and then all the way to 8:00 without one person walking through the doors asking about the concert, Dora and I slowly realized that this concert would definitely not be generating much benefit to the school, if any. Winston came by around 8:05 to see what was happening. I gave him the bad news that no tickets had been sold and it didn't look like there would be many late comers either. He seemed to take it in stride and told us to wait a little longer before abandoning our post. After he left we sat there until almost 8:30 and then we decided it was time to abandon ship.

The comedian and the Chief had shown up shortly after we had arrived and were sitting in the open cafeteria area next to the snack bar just outside the hockey arena entrance. We walked down to join them and drink some coffee while we waited for Winston to come out and officially cancel the show. Instead, around 9:00 pm, the lead singer for one of the acts stuck his head out the door and said, enthusiastically "Well, are you guys ready?"

I'm sure he was expecting an energetic response, but we were all pretty much resigned to the fact that this whole thing was turning into a horrendous dud and we were just waiting to be released. The singer wouldn't let it die a quiet death, however and urged us all to come into the arena. "Come on! We're gonna have a show anyway!" he said.

Yolande and the rest of the group and I looked at each other with that "oh, well" expression on our faces and slowly got up to go into the arena. We were going to have to have fun whether we wanted to or not!

Under any other circumstances, the show would have probably been considered good. But because there were approximately 8 of us, including the facility staff, sitting in a darkened arena with over 300 seats set up in front of a stage where 3 different country and western bands would be playing, along with a comedian, it all seemed pretty sad. We watched the opening act and clapped dutifully after each song was finished, and I have to admit, they were really good musicians. It still seemed surreal to be the only people watching the show, but the term "captive audience" was never more appropriate than there. Nobody really wanted to stay for another two hours, but we all knew how hopeful Winston had been about this, so we stayed so as not to make it seem any worse. Beside, we had to see Winston sing his song in traditional ceremonial make-up!

Finally around 11:00 p.m., the bands took a brief intermission and Dora told me her cousin, the Chief needed to leave because it was very late and he was very tired. She had ridden in with us and said she didn't trust herself to find the house in the dark, so could we drive back to the house so they could follow us? This seemed like an excellent way to bail out, even though the comedian and one other band had not yet performed, so we said sure.

As it turned out, the comedian wasn't willing to go onstage and try to do comedy in front of 4 or 5 people, so he decided he would ride along with Dora and the Chief. Even though we had only been there once earlier that day I was sure I knew how to get back to the house, so I got into my car and led the way.

Everything went fine until we got to the main exit into Peace River. I didn't realize it was the last exit before the road to Coyote Lake, so I had to pull over, get out and walk back to Dora's car to tell her how I would try to get back to the house. We turned around and headed back into town to find the right exit. We succeeded in doing this, but then we had to find the mountain road that led up to the summit.

Getting onto the road was no problem, but as we were driving up the steep winding grade, I realized that the driveway would be much harder to find at night than during the day. None of the landmarks and houses along the way could be seen in the darkness, and I had been so preoccupied with trying to follow Winston that afternoon, I probably wouldn't have recognized them anyway. We drove slowly up the gravel road, looking for the driveway. All we could see were trees and bushes on either side of the unlit road. It seemed like were going a lot farther than we did in the afternoon, but without any signs or visual aids we couldn't tell for sure. Finally we got all the way to the top of the hill and started going down the other side. I knew for sure we had overshot our target, so I pulled over and walked back to Dora's car again.

"Well, I guess you probably realized we must have passed it up, right?" Dora just looked at me blankly and I realized she was very confused. I tried to assure her that we just had to backtrack until we found the driveway.

I got into my car and headed back up towards the summit. Again, Yo and I searched the side of the road to find the driveway and again we couldn't find it. We went all the way down to the foot of the hill again, where I pulled over and walked back to talk to Dora one more time. I was beginning to feel very embarrassed because I had told Dora she could follow me and really thought I knew how to get back. Now, I was just as confused as anyone and I admitted to Dora, the Chief and the comedian. "OK, I give up! Anyone else got any suggestions?"

The comedian claimed he knew we were on the right road and that we had to go back up it again to find the driveway. Dora just looked at me blankly.

"OK," I said. "I'll just keep looking. If anyone has any better ideas, feel free to let me know."

We drove back up into the darkness and this time, miraculously found the elusive driveway. We pulled into the mini-mansion and got out of our cars with a sigh of relief. It was a good lesson, though. There weren't a lot of well-lit roads in that part of Alberta, so if you were going to drive somewhere at night, you'd better know where you're going!

The next day we all got up late and made arrangements to meet back at the house in time to go to the arena for the second show that night. Y and I drove back to Coyote Lake to witness the last day of Treaty Days and then made the drive back to the house to pick up the comedian before we returned to the arena. Dora and the Chief had decided they didn't need to stick around to see the concert again, so they left to go back to British Columbia. Yo, the comedian and I drove back to the arena, hoping that there would be a least a few customers for the second night.

No such luck. Once again, the fund raiser was a total bomb! One couple actually showed up about a half hour before the doors opened and told us that someone had given them their tickets (apparently they were tickets that were supposed to be given away by one of the radio stations). When they found out that they would be the only ones in the audience, however, they decided to bail out. So once again, Winston put on an entire concert and paid the bands and the comedian (even though he never went onstage) out of his own money, and didn't even get one paying customer. The comedian got a ride out of town directly from the arena, so Yo and I were able to go back to the house and gratefully spend the night alone.

So ended Treaty Days, and my first assignment as a volunteer. It was really sad, from my point of view that Winston worked so hard to raise some money for the school and came up empty. I didn't think anything could be any worse than that.

I would soon find out, however, that I was wrong.

****

During the first week after the concert debacle Yo and I made the 45 minute drive into Coyote Lake every day and went off to our respective "jobs". Yo had been drafted to serve as the emergency substitute second grade teacher for the reservation school until a permanent replacement could be found. Although she had planned on being simply a teacher's assistant, without any responsibility for planning lessons and taking control of a class, the school principal practically begged her to hold the fort until a suitable replacement arrived. She wasn't exactly crazy about the idea, but the principal promised her it would be a temporary fix, so she reluctantly agreed.

For the first Sunday after the concert and for the rest of the following week, Yo spent a good three days trying to re-organize her classroom, which had been left in a state of complete disorganization by the prior teachers. She found duplicate packages of art supplies which had never been opened in the cabinets, magazine which sere supposedly gathered for art projects from seven or eight years prior and a total lack of logic in the way the room had been arranged. I spent the better part of the first weekend after the concerts and before the school had officially opened joining her in her classroom, not so much to help organize it, since I had no idea how she wanted it set up, but more to keep her company. In addition, I tried to help her scrounge chairs from the school gymnasium where two or three dozen had been waiting for the last two months since the school shut down for the summer in June. It was truly amazing to see how much wastefulness had been allowed to take place over the previous years in the form of unnecessary textbooks and duplicate supplies, etc. for a school that apparently so poor that it was a struggle to find enough money to pay the teachers willing to come to such a backwoods post.

I, on the other hand, would simply drop Yo off at the school entrance each morning and then drive around to Winston's house on the other side of the fairgrounds field. Then I would enter the front door and sit down at the kitchen table next to Winston, who was already busy answering emails or reading text messages from his myriad of business partners. We would talk for a few minutes or I would sit and wait for him to finish his phone call. At a few minutes before 9:00 a.m., Winston would let me know he was ready to go and we would walk over to the band office a few hundred yards away.

We would walk into the band office and after the first two or three times we would take off our shoes just inside the door before walking back to Winston's offices. The reason for this was because the roads inside the reservation were all unpaved and after the end of summer, they were almost always covered with mud, so it kept the floors a lot cleaner if everyone went shoeless.

There was a reception area inside the main entrance and there were always 4 or 5 people sitting in the lobby, drinking coffee and eating donuts or sweet rolls. Winston would usually introduce me to two or three people, tell me what they did in the band, tell them that I was a volunteer from California, and then we walked away.

I know I almost instantly forgot the names of the people Winston introduced me too and wondered if they instantly forgot who I was too. It didn't seem to matter since once I had been introduced to any of these people, I almost never saw or spoke to them again.

Once we had walked through the gauntlet of people sitting in the reception area, Winston and I walked to his tiny office in the rear of the building. Ironically enough, it was right across the hall from the office where his nemesis Matthew worked. Winston would plug in his laptop and start reading and sending more emails or reading more text messages or making more phone calls while I sat and waited to find out what I was supposed to do. I could tell Winston didn't like to be rushed and didn't follow any type of strict schedule unless he had a meeting scheduled, so I tried to be patient and wait until he had finished whatever urgent business he had to deal with it. After an hour or so, I started to get tired of waiting and asked Winston if we had anything scheduled to do that day. "Yes, yes!" he said "We're going to start working on some grant requests, but for the first week or so, I just want you to listen and watch so you can get a good idea of the procedures and the protocol we go through. It will take a little time, so just be patient and give yourself a week or so to get used to the routine here."

That sounded reasonable, so I wasn't too concerned when the first day consisted of mostly watching and listening to Winston taking phone calls and reading emails and occasionally talking to a band member or one of the elders who dropped in to say hello and find out if Winston had any new business opportunities they might be able to be involved in. Watching and listening seemed pretty simple, and I needed something else to do to keep me busy, so I usually checked my emails and surfed the net on my laptop while I was waiting for something to happen. The second day in the band office was pretty much a repeat of the first day. The third day was similar to the last and the next day was pretty much the same as well.

Pretty soon this inactivity became fairly routine and except for a few meetings with oil company representatives and others here and there, each day became a repeat of the last day and then each week became a repeat of the last week. By the end of the first three weeks, it appeared that my job was simply to function as a goodwill ambassador without any real duties and no real schedule other than to sit alongside Winston in his office every day and wait for him to find something for me to do. Every time I would ask him if we had any proposals to write or any meetings to prepare for, the answer was always the same. Yes, yes, he would say, we were going to start putting together a proposal right after lunch, or as soon he finished a letter he was writing, or as soon as he made another phone call, or had a meeting with Chief Tyson, or had a chat with one of the band who just stopped into his office, etc., etc., etc.

In between all the activities he was doing that appeared to be related to official band business, Winston received a number of calls from friends and associates from some of his personal businesses which did not seem to be related to the band's business in any way. Still, I was there for the long haul and figured I might as well try to get used to how things worked on the reservation, like Winston told me to do, and not worry too much about not getting much done. Still, it was undeniably boring and sometimes it actually became a struggle to stay awake while sitting in the office during the afternoon.

Yolande in the meantime had inherited a group of fifth graders with an academic competence below the third graders she had taught in Chile. Some of the students seemed to deliberately sit at their desks and do almost nothing all day long. The culture in the reservation did not seem to put a very high priority on education, and most of the students had little interest in learning anything and felt no need to pretend they did. As a result, Yolande also spent many frustrating days trying to teach students who, for the most part, weren't interested in learning, with no real recourse to get them to make an effort. Similare to Chile, there was no real discipline system in place. Sending the student to the principal's office was not available because the principal felt that he should not have to do with discipline problems. Therefore the teachers were left on their own to deal with students who had severe learning problems and who had almost no motivation to try to improve. Yo had to try to teach her lessons at an agonizingly slow pace, so her frustration level was increasing on a daily basis too. When I picked her up at the end of her school day for the 45 minute drive back to Tyson's house in Peace River we would compare notes to see who had the most frustrating day. As boring and unproductive as my day was, her days usually sounded even worse.

During one of the first few days at the band office, Winston introduced me to Thomas. Thomas was a young recent college graduate who had been functioning as Winston's assistant for the three months prior to our arrival in Coyote Lake. He was not a full Aboriginal, or First Nations citizen because he was only half "Indian" and half something else, which meant he was what was called a "Metis". On top of that, he was also Chief Tyson's younger brother. He was actually the only young person working in the band office, but he was planning on leaving the reservation shortly to take a trip to Europe and then resume his education. He was very friendly and well spoken, and after talking with him for a few minutes and finding out what he had been doing with Winston for the past few months, it became clear to me, that I was actually there to take Thomas' place after he left the band.

After we chatted for a little while, Winston suggested we all take a ride in his car to see the band in the next town called Running Bison, and to meet some of the band members there. When we got there, several band members were working furiously on the school building, painting walls, moving desks and furniture, installing lamps and fixtures, etc. We were told that their school was opening the next day and they were trying to get it ready for the students to use. It looked to me like it wouldn't be ready for a week, but as usual, I kept my comments to myself. The last thing I wanted to do was give off a negative impression.

After visiting the school, Winston drove through the forest to a dirt road that led to a small lake. We all got out of the car and Winston pointed out various types of trees and plants to me. Thomas mentioned that this was the area that he had grown up in and came to fish at this lake many times as a youth.

There didn't seem to be any real reason for us to take this trip and I once again came to the conclusion that Winston had decided that this was just a way to kill some time. It was beautiful scenery, but at the same time, I couldn't help wondering if the rest of our ten month assignment was actually going to be as boring and insignificant as the first two weeks had been. At one point, Thomas took me aside while Winston was busy talking to someone on his cell phone and warned me that Winston had to be monitored and continually "re-focused" in order to get anything done. He admitted that he, too had spent most of his time sitting and waiting for Winston to assign some duties to him and ultimately found things to do on his own. He told me that Winston was truly a good guy and really wanted to help his people become self-sufficient and break the cycle of oppression they had lived under for over a hundred years, but he was extremely undisciplined and did things according to his own schedule.

I thanked him for his insight, even though I didn't know how it would change anything. Yo and I were still in the backwoods of Alberta, Canada, waiting to find out what we were supposed to do that would be anything close to what we were told our duties would be (i.e. assisting the school's teachers for her and assisting the CEO of the Economic Development Department of the band in preparing grant requests and business plans), On top of that we were going to be there for over nine more months.

The good news was that eventually the school had to find a permanent replacement to teach Yo's class and eventually Winston had to give me something to do that would actually help improve the economic situation for the people in the band, but exactly when it would happen was anybody's guess. At least we were living out another unique experience which we were sure would eventually result in some benefit to the First Nations people we were working for, and all our living expenses (food, lodging, health insurance, winter clothing and car expenses) would be reimbursed by the band, so we wouldn't make any money from the assignment, but we wouldn't lose any either.

Or at least that's what we thought.

Around the middle of my third week on Coyote Lake, Winston asked me if I would like to join him at a conference for several First Nation bands at a resort hotel in the south of British Columbia for a few days. He was going to be a guest speaker, as was Chief Tyson, and he showed me a glossy brochure that listed a thumbnail sketch of all the speakers on the program and the seminars and workshops planned for the three day meeting. In addition, it would be held in a four star resort hotel with a heated pool, exercise room, and gourmet meals, all provided by the Wild Hawk First Nation. Since it sounded a lot more interesting than sitting in Winston's office for three days pretending to have something to do, of course I said yes!

Thomas, Winston's ex-assistant and Chief Tyson's brother happened to be in the office that day. He was supposed to order business cards for me, but had not done so yet, because I didn't have a cell phone number for him to list. Winston had advised me to wait until coming to Canada to buy a cell phone, because it would be cheaper and easier to do it there and we could also avoid any tariff charges. After three weeks, Winston still hadn't taken any action to order the phone, and I had to leave it up to him because it was something the band was supposed to pay for. Although I reminded him about this several times, he always responded the same way. "Yeah, I'll take care of it!" As Thomas told me, you had to have extreme patience when it came to dealing with Winston. He always seemed to be dealing with several different issues, most of them related to his own business dealings and my concerns were usually near the very bottom of his priorities.

A little before noon one day, Winston looked at Thomas and me and said "Let's go get some lunch!" This was our signal that Winston was done making phone calls, answering emails or chatting with people in the band office for the morning and was ready to treat us to lunch in his own kitchen. We walked over to his house, but before he started making his usual soup or sandwiches, he announced that he had brought back some delicacies from his trip to the conference in British Columbia. Among the delicacies were dried salmon, caribou meat and "muktuk". I asked him what "muktuk" was and he advised that it was dried whale blubber and it was a taste sensation I wouldn't want to miss. I didn't want to look like a sissified white boy to my two Aboriginal friends, so I unwrapped a chunk of the solid white meat and took a few bites.

I won't say that it was the worst thing I ever tasted, but it had to be in the top five. Of course, I didn't tell this to Winston or Thomas, who downed a couple of chunks and said "Not bad!" I just politely swallowed the piece I had been chewing for about five minutes and muttered something like "Hmmm! That's different!"

"Isn't it delicious?" Winston asked me. I just smiled and said, "Well, it might take a little getting used to."

"Oh, man!" he said. "I love this stuff! I can't get enough of it! We used to eat it all the time up in the Arctic!" I mentally crossed off any plans for a trip to the Arctic if this was the only kind of food they had there. I manfully finished the last piece of my muktuk and tried to find something to wash it down. I eventually found some bread to make a sandwich with and tried some of the dried salmon. Not exactly something I would go out of my way to find, but at least it was better than the muktuk.

I wasn't able to satisfy my hunger with this lunch, but I couldn't force myself to eat any more of it either. Thomas seemed to be overcome with sleepiness after he finished his two or three pieces of muktuk and promptly stretched out on the sofa in

Winston's den to take a nap. I sat and surfed the internet while Winston finished making some more calls while my stomach slowly gurgled.

We went back to the band office after lunch where we continued the daily drone routine. I sat and searched for something to do on the internet while Winston read proposals, wrote emails, made phone calls and said "Yes, we're going to get to that!" after I asked him if there were any projects or proposals we could work on. Within a minute or two he would follow this up by saying "Just as soon as I...", and then he would get lost in another email, phone call, letter or conference with one of the band members who dropped in to chat. All during this time, my stomach started gurgling more and what I thought was heartburn started hitting me every half hour or so.

After Yo and I got back to Tyson's house that night, the heartburn became seriously worse. I could feel waves of pain starting in my lower stomach that seemed to roll up through my torso until they reached my chest. Then they would disappear for around five minutes before they would start again. Although I wasn't really hungry, I tried to eat some "normal" food to see if that would make it go away. Unfortunately, that seemed to only make it worse and more intense. When it came time to go to bed, I found that trying to lie down started the whole process up again, making it impossible to sleep.

This went on for almost the whole night. Even though I only had about an hour's sleep, the next morning I had to drive Yo all the way into town around 45 minutes away so that she could teach her class. All during this time, the pain and nausea kept getting stronger. After I dropped Yo off I went over to Winston's house as usual and informed him that I didn't think I would be able to make the trip to the conference the next day. He said he understood and advised me to just take it easy for the next few days and wait until he returned. I really hated having to miss the conference, since it would at least provide some activity, and I couldn't take it any *easier* than I had for the last three weeks, but if I was going to be sick, it was probably better that I stayed there. No matter how bad I felt while I was there, it probably wouldn't be any better on the road.

Shortly after noon, I was able to pick Yo up and drive back to the house because classes finished early that day for some reason. By the time we got back to Peace River the pain was almost continuous. I gulped down almost a whole bottle of Pepto Bismol and eventually succeeded in making myself vomit. That seemed to help for a little while, but within an hour the whole process started all over again.

I couldn't eat, I couldn't sleep, and I couldn't lie down for about 24 hours. It was the most painful illness I think I'd ever been through. I thought I might have to check myself into a hospital, which presented a whole list of potential problems, since I wasn't sure how the charity's health insurance worked, but then I never imagined I'd be needing it for a hospital stay. On top of that, I didn't really know where the nearest hospital was, although I knew I could find it with the chamber of commerce map we had, assuming I could manage to drive myself down the gravel mountain road to the emergency room in the dark.

After what seemed like an eternity, the pains finally subsided and I found I was able to eat small amounts of solid food again. Eventually the pain and heartburn went away after over a day and a half of pure misery. I vowed then and there never to eat anything Winston recommended on the basis that he loved it when he lived in the Arctic. Muktuk might be a treat for Native Americans and polar bears, but it almost killed me!

Before Winston went away to his conference, he told me I was going to be working with the band manager for a few days to help her set up their accounting system while he was gone. It seemed that the band had an annual audit that they had to complete in order to maintain the government funding they received, and it was supposed to be wrapped up that week. Winston told me he felt that the band manager, who was in charge of the financial reports was at best incompetent, and at worst guilty of misappropriating band funds. He told me that this was a common occurrence in the Canadian reservations and that a recent audit in the next closest reservation had uncovered about 15 million dollars in funds under the chief's control which had not been accounted for.

15 million dollars!!!

He suspected that the reason the band manager was so uncooperative with him was because she feared he might be able to detect a similar problem.

I never realized the amount of money passing through the First Nations reservations from the oil, gas and pipeline companies in return for being able to extract all their natural resources was so large, so this was something of an eye opener. Winston said the corruption among First Nations band leaders in Alberta was especially bad because Alberta had more untapped oil and gas reserves than any other province in Canada. He said the pattern was for a few of the band leaders to pocket small fortunes for themselves and their families and siphon the money off into family owned businesses, like construction companies, trucking companies, etc. so that they could provide a steady income for themselves and their loved ones while the rest of the band just barely survived. Yolande later confirmed that several of the kids she taught at the res school appeared to be unable to afford warm winter clothing because they often came to school wearing only a thin shirt and summer jacket or sweater after the weather had turned cold, and there was already snow on the ground in late September.

In spite of his suspicions, or maybe because of it, Winston somehow arranged for me to work with the band manager for about week or so, ostensibly to help her process the band's bookkeeping, but probably more to give me something to do while he was gone. He had introduced me to her late one afternoon a few days before he left. For obvious reasons, I won't mention her real name here. Let's call her Martha.

Martha seemed fairly reasonable the day I met her and when I asked what she wanted me to do, she asked me to meet with her early the next day because she was still busy with the outside auditor, trying to get the band's annual audit done. I met with her the next day and after a short interview in which I discussed my background with her, she seemed fairly impressed and said she thought I could be of some help to her. She told me that she worked at the band office as the band manager from 9:00 to 5:00 every day and then after dinner came back to work until 9:00 or 10:00 every night to "fix the mistakes" that her bookkeepers made during the day.

I asked her if she showed the bookkeepers the mistakes they made and explained how it should be done correctly. She said yes, she did, but the next day they would forget what she had shown them and go back to making the same mistakes again.

I thought it was a little strange that she didn't replace a bookkeeper who was obviously incompetent, but then I realized she probably couldn't. Everybody in the band office was related to one of the band elders or officers, and they probably couldn't be fired no matter how many mistakes they made. This was probably one of the main reasons that incompetence and inefficiency seemed to flourish. Martha asked me if I could spend some time with the bookkeepers and teach them how the books were supposed to be kept and I of course agreed. Then she gave me some pamphlets that described the accounting program they were using and asked me to begin with the Accounts Payable module since that was the one that seemed to always have the most errors involved. I spent the rest of the afternoon reading through the documentation and waiting for a signal to begin working with the bookkeeping staff.

The signal never came and at the end of the day I asked her if she wanted me to work with her staff the next day and where did she want me to sit, etc. She said she hadn't been able to discuss it with her staff and wanted to tell them what was happening first, so she asked me to wait until tomorrow to begin. No problem I told her.

The next day I asked her where she wanted me to work and she set up a PC on a desk in the main office area, just outside the bookkeepers' office. I spent a short time reviewing some of the screens on line and waited for Martha to come back to let me know what she wanted me to start on. When she didn't come back by noon, I began to search for her, but she was nowhere to be found. I couldn't find her in the afternoon either, but finally found her outside the building taking a cigarette break with the bookkeeper who was supposedly causing so much trouble.

I overheard them talking about the expense reports that I had submitted before Winston left for his trip. The bookkeeper said "If they're volunteers, why should we pay them anything?" This was a bit disturbing since Winston and the charity organization's recruiter had assured me our living expenses would be completely reimbursed. "The oil company gave us a $50,000 grant to cover all their expenses, but you know what happened to that," Martha told her. "That got used up to pay for the bounce house during Treaty Days!"

They both got a good laugh out of this. I didn't think it was all that funny.

I finally got close enough to interrupt them. "Martha, did you want me to work on any payables this afternoon?"

She looked a little startled to see me, perhaps because she might have realized I had heard what they were talking about. "Ummm…no I think we should wait until tomorrow. We're still trying to get all our loose ends tied up from the audit, so give me until tomorrow to get it all organized for you."

Fine, I said. I'll see you tomorrow.

The next day was basically a repeat of the prior one. The desk where I had my PC set up to start working on the accounting system had been relocated and there was no place to plug in the PC anymore. On top of that Martha was nowhere to be found again. I decided to go back to Winston's office and wait for her to come find me when she was ready to show me what she needed me to do. The clock ticked away and by the end of the day, she still hadn't appeared. I went to her office to try to find her and she was gone for the day.

I was beginning to understand why Winston was so frustrated with Martha and felt she was uncooperative, but in all truthfulness, my days with him weren't any more productive. It seemed like I had somehow been sentenced to some type of minimum security prison, with little to do except wait for my jail term to be up.

At one point I had been concerned that she expected me to be an accounting clerk, simply entering invoices into the Accounts Payable module because she had mentioned she thought I could help them get caught up within the next three months. Now it seemed like she didn't know what she wanted me to do, so I figured I would just bide my time until Winston came back, and then hopefully we would finally start doing something meaningful.

The morning after Winston returned from his conference, I came to Winston's house to start our usual glacially-paced routine. I was surprised that he answered the door in his bathrobe, but he told me that he was just too sick to go to the office that day. Apparently, giving his speech at the conference, hob-nobbing with the oil company representatives and other attendees, and driving the 8 hour commute back and forth took a lot out of him. I was sorry to hear this, not only because I didn't want him to feel sickly, especially with the memory of my muktuk ordeal still fresh in my mind, but also because I wanted to get my expense reimbursement.

When Yolande and I initially contacted the charity about volunteering with them they let us know the terms of the assignment would be that we were reimbursed for all our living expenses (food, lodging, winter clothing, health insurance, travel expenses and $50 pocket money per week), but we would not be paid any salary or get any other reimbursement. This was fine with us, but we never asked exactly HOW we would be reimbursed for these expenses. I didn't know if we would get a weekly allowance, whether all our food would be prepared for us, or if we were supposed to submit expense reports with receipts for reimbursement. When I called the chief recruiter that we had spoken to initially, he advised that it was something that the band would handle and told me to discuss it with Winston. Of course, whenever I asked Winston about it he would say "Don't worry about it. I'll take care of it." After hearing this 4 or 5 times I finally let him know that we had over $2,000 in expenses that needed to be reimbursed and we were running low on funds. He finally was able to obtain an expense report form from the band office and told me to fill it out and submit it with our receipts.

I had done this over a week and a half earlier, but still could not get an answer from Winston as to when it would be paid. He usually told me something like he had discussed it with the band manager and it was *her* fault that it hadn't been paid yet.

Around this time, I began to realize that several of the band members were not very fond of Winston. I already knew there was bad blood between him and Matthew, the Environmental Manager, and Winston had also told me that he and the band office manager were not on good terms, mostly because he felt she was either incompetent or dishonest, or both. In any event, the meter kept ticking and our expenses kept increasing every week, so I had told Winston we had to get some money reimbursed or else we would have to abandon the assignment.

Of course, he told me that that wouldn't be necessary because the band had already received enough money form the oil company that was sponsoring our volunteer assignment as a goodwill gesture to cover twice as much expenses as we could possibly generate in 10 months. I answered that that all sounded good on paper, but the fact was that we had been there nearly four weeks already and still had no reimbursements to show for any of our expenses. He then told me he to list all our expenses since arriving, plus our travel expenses within Canada on a spread sheet and he would personally bring it to Chief Tyson's attention after he returned from the conference in B.C.

Now that the day had come when he was back and we could finally meet with Chief Tyson to get our expenses paid, Winston said he was too sick to go to the office to take care of it. "But you can talk to Tyson yourself. He's a good guy! He'll make sure you get paid! Just tell him you have to have the money or you'll have to go back to California!"

OK, great. I'll go talk to Tyson myself. Thanks for all your help, Winston!

I walked over to the band office and asked the receptionist if Chief Tyson was in. He was there, she said, but he was in the middle of a meeting. I asked her to tell him I needed to see him when he was done and went to Winston's office to wait.

After about an hour or so, I got tired of surfing the net and decided it was time to try again. This time the receptionist said he was in but didn't know where he went. I decided to just walk through the door and risk barging in on him to try to get an answer once and for all.

I walked through the door, down the hall to the waiting room, just outside all the band council's' offices. He was actually just coming out of someone else's office when he saw me. "Hi, Michael! You wanted to see me? OK, come on into my office."

I went into Tyson's office and sat down. I started off with a lame joke about how I was finally able to come inside the "sacred chambers". He gave out a small chuckle, and I began to show him the spreadsheets I had prepared showing our travel expenses for driving to the reservation from the Canadian border and also for all our living expenses we had incurred during the three and a half weeks since we arrived.

I was beginning to present my case by saying "I really hate to be a whiner, and I'm sure this isn't the biggest problem you have to deal with, but…". Before I could finish he cut me off.

"Is Winston here today?"

"No, he said he was too sick to come in."

Tyson closed his eyes and raised his hand to his forehead.

"I have to tell you something in complete confidence," he said.

I stopped and waited. "Okay", I said. "Whatever it is I'll keep it to myself."

"Winston is getting fired."

"*Excuse* me?"

"Winston is getting fired. The band leaders just had a vote and none of them are willing to work with him anymore. I thought I could sway them into going along with him, but they wouldn't agree to it. I have to carry out their wishes."

I was almost too stunned to speak. I couldn't believe that this was happening two days after both Winston and Tyson had come back from speaking at the conference in B.C. together. More importantly, though, I was actually more concerned about whether or not Yo and I were expected to continue working for the band without Winston for the next 9 months. I was waiting to hear Tyson say something like "Don't worry! We still want you and Yolande to stay and keep working with us. Yolande can keep teaching in the school, and you can still work in the office, but Winston has to go."

But that's not what he said. Instead he said "I'm really sorry. I know it's a mess, but there's nothing I can do about it."

Wow. Talk about a slap in the face! I sat there for a few moments before I finally was able to ask about our expense reimbursements.

"Yes, I know. We will pay you for all your expenses, In fact I just approved the spreadsheets you emailed to me, so you should get a check for the total amount due by the end of the week."

Okay. That took care of the expenses, I thought, but what were Yolande and I supposed to do now? We had quit our jobs, terminated our apartment lease, sold off or gave away most of our furniture and only had a few dozen boxes of clothes, mementos and household goods in storage left. We had planned on being in Alberta for 10 months minimum and now it looked like we had to find a new place to live and another occupation after only a month!

I kept waiting for Tyson say "Of course, we are not going to make you leave. We can find something useful for you to do here."

Nope. He didn't say it. He just sat there staring at me like he knew he had just sentenced us to death, or at least to life in prison. It didn't look like begging would do any good at this point, and besides, I didn't really know what it was I had been brought there to do anyway. Winston had been telling me for nearly four weeks we were going to start preparing proposals for government grants and write up business plans to develop the economy on the res, but he never actually got around to it. All I had really done was to sit and take notes at two or three meetings with oil and pipeline company reps regarding reparations for oil spills and watch Winston chat on the phone, read emails and bluster about how the band manager and some of the other band leaders couldn't understand how much good he was doing for them. So now Yolande and I were getting the heave-ho along with our boss because the band didn't really like him, and from what I had gathered, never really wanted him there in the first place.

"Does Winston know this?" I asked.

"No," Tyson said. "That's why I need you to keep this in confidence until I tell him."

"Well, when are you going to tell him?"

He looked a bit nervous for a few seconds, but then he said "I guess I'll go and tell him right now."

With that he got up from his chair and walked out of his office. I sat there for a few moments, not knowing exactly what to do. Finally I walked back to Winston's office and spent another hour or so surfing the net, waiting for Tyson to deliver the bad news before I went to ask Winston what the hell we were supposed to do now.

He called out "Come in!" when I knocked on the door, and after I walked in he certainly didn't seem upset. I wondered if Tyson actually spoke to him, so I asked "Did Tyson come here to talk to you?"

"Oh, yeah, he was here."

"So...did he tell you you were....fired?" I asked tentatively.

"He tried, but he changed his mind after I told him I would sue him and the band if they tried to do it. I've got a contract to serve as the CEO for the Economic Development team, and I'm not going to let them kick me out because a few greedy council members don't like me. He decided to take his termination papers back and he'll have to talk to the council again to make them understand what they're dealing with!"

He sounded super confident and I thought he sounded so sure of himself that he had to be right. Apparently, his contract must have had a no termination clause and the band was now stuck with him whether they liked it or not. Wow! This was another unexpected turn of events!

"Really? You mean they can't get rid of you?" I asked.

"No, not the way I understand it," he said. (Uh oh!) "I'm going to have my attorney review it, but I don't think they have a leg to stand on. If they want to get rid of me they're going to have to reimburse me for all the expenses I paid out for this band, including the $80,000 I spent on those concerts!"

$80,000! I had no idea he spent that much money on those two debacles that nobody came to! I knew Winston had a lot of money, but I didn't realize he could afford to spend that much on something so uncertain as the benefit concerts he staged. Well, then, maybe he could afford a lawyer who could fight this and preserve all our assignments with the band.

However, when I asked what we should plan on doing for the next few days, he immediately started to backtrack.

"Well. I think we should just lay low for the next two or three days while I decide exactly what I should do," he said.

Huh? I thought you just got done saying you were going to fight it?

"Yeah, but I have to find out what's the best way to do it. I'm not even 100% sure I want to fight it. I've gotten so much shit from these people that maybe I'd be better off just leaving and let them screw up all the opportunities I set up for them with the grant proposals I submitted. They don't even understand the potential they have to help their own people! But they don't really care about anybody else! They just want to grab as much money as they can for themselves!"

I had no doubt that what Winston was saying was true, but I still didn't have any idea about what he was really planning to do – and since Yo and I had uprooted our whole lives to come to work there for 10 months I felt like we deserved an answer.

"Here's what I think we should do," he finally said. "Don't say anything to your wife about it tonight or tomorrow, because I don't want her to say anything to Donna yet". (Donna was Winston's wife who also taught at the school in a classroom right across the hall from Yolande.) "Let's let things settle down a little and we'll see what happens and then we'll decide what we're going to do on Monday."

It seemed reasonable enough, since it was then a Thursday evening, and Yo and I could wait until Monday to find out what our fate with the Wild Hawk would be. So we spent a relatively nervous weekend at Chief Tyson's house in Peace River (he had promised he wouldn't kick us out until we had made arrangements to transfer someplace else). On Monday I returned to Winston's house expecting a decision about what was going to happen with Winston and Donna and Yolande and me.

To my surprise, Winston told me that he and Donna hadn't made a decision yet and we would all have to have a meeting to discuss what was best "for all of us" at his house that evening after supper. I spent the day sitting at Winston's kitchen table doing the same thing I had done with him in his office over the past 4 weeks – listening to him make phone calls, read emails and now rant about how stupid and selfish the band council was and how they would be sorry about how screwed up things would be once he was gone.

Finally Yolande and Donna walked into the house after the school day was finished around 4:30 that afternoon. We all ate the food Winston had prepared for us and then Donna started the ball rolling by asking us what we thought about what had happened.

What did we think? I thought to myself. *We think it's a bloody mess and we'd like to know how you're going to fix it!*

The basic problem was Winston didn't know exactly what he wanted to do, even though he kept saying he had plenty of business opportunities to go to elsewhere, and Donna wasn't sure she wanted to give up teaching at the school. Yolande also wasn't exactly happy about the prospect of leaving the school. She had just recently convinced the principal that she had not signed on to be a full time teacher and would be quitting whether or not he found a replacement within the next week or so. The principal had informed her only a few days earlier that he definitely had a replacement for her, but he just needed her to stay there one more week to allow the replacement to arrive. After that she could work on organizing the library or assisting the other teachers with art projects and assisting with arranging games for the kids during recess, etc., etc. like she had always wanted to do. Now that she was finally on the verge of being able to do the kind of work she wanted to do at the school, it appeared that we would have to leave.

Now it sounded like Winston had decided he didn't want to continue working with the band after all, but he couldn't decide if he and Donna would stay in Coyote Lake so she could keep teaching school there, or if he should relocate and allow Donna to stay there with Winston returning on weekends. Or if they should both call it quits and move someplace else. They both felt like they had to mull it over a little while longer before making any decisions. "After all," Donna told us "it's our *careers!*"

"Yeah, I know," I told her," but it's *our* careers too!" I felt like she thought that because we were working as volunteers that we could be expected to put our lives on hold while she and Winston decided what would work out best for them. I didn't want to be stuck in Limbo any longer than I had to. "Oh, yes, I know," she said," but it's still something that takes time to decide."

"Don't worry, Michael, no matter what happens we'll get another assignment for you and Yolande soon!" Winston chimed in. "You could work at one of the other reservations up around the Arctic, if you can handle the cold, or there's another opportunity to work with another First Nations group in Edmonton, or we might find a job for you and Yolande to work for the foundation in Toronto. That's where their headquarters are, and they could probably find something for volunteers to do in the home office. It all depends on what you think you'd like to do!"

I wasn't crazy about the thought of working and living in the Arctic, especially since winter was about to start, but working on another assignment in Edmonton or Toronto sounded interesting. I spoke to Yo about it on the way back to Tyson's house that evening and she basically felt the same way.

The next day I came to work in Winston's kitchen again and told him that Yo and I had discussed our options and felt that either Edmonton or Toronto would be the best fit for us. Winston agreed, but he said "It might be better if we can find an assignment for you in Edmonton. Toronto is a great place to live, but I think it might take a lot longer to find positions that both you and Yolande could work at there. But I've got some contacts with a Metis group in Edmonton that I think would work out for you, so let's try that route first. It might take a week or so, but just be patient and I'll try to get it set up!"

Be patient? *Be patient??* I almost wanted to scream! We had been in Canada for almost 5 weeks by then and I still hadn't done anything that would qualify as working on the "Economic Development Team" other than take notes and listen to Winston jabber the day away for almost the whole day, every day of the work week. On top of that, I now had about $3,000 of expenses that *still* hadn't been paid. This was turning into a full blown catastrophe and I tried my best to be patient and understanding, but I also told

Winston that we had to get something soon or we would just have to go back to the U.S. and look for a "real job" again.

The next week I came to Winston's house on Monday morning to continue sitting around for most of the day, trying to find something to do while waiting for Winston to come up with a new assignment for us. Unfortunately, his front door was locked and there was no answer when I knocked or rang the bell. I drove back to the school where I had dropped Yolande off just a few minutes earlier and walked into Donna's classroom to ask if she knew where her husband was.

She smiled at me when I walked into her room and handed me her set of keys. "I guess you probably need these to get in the house," she said.

Yes, I said, and I also wanted to know where Winston was.

"Oh, he's out of town. He won't be back until Wednesday."

Then she gave me her keys and started teaching the kids in her class a lesson. I guess she figured that was all I needed to know. I went back to Winston's house and seethed for the next two days waiting to find out what we would be doing with the rest of our lives.

On Wednesday, Winston still wasn't back home. When I went to her classroom to get the keys again, Donna told me she wasn't sure when he would be back, but possibly not until Friday.

All this time I was trying desperately not to lose my mind from the boredom of having absolutely nothing to do all day. I tried emailing Winston, but he often took days to respond to any emails. I tried calling him once or twice, but apparently he was somewhere where his cell phone was out of range. By Thursday afternoon, I was getting near the end of my patience and I sent Winston a relatively angry email explaining why I thought we had been misled into coming there and had to get an answer about where we would be working soon or we would have to head back to California and try to start over there.

He finally answered my call late Thursday and said he understood why I was frustrated and that he was working on a potential assignment with the Metis group in Edmonton and that he just needed a few more days get it arranged

"Be patient," he said. *"Be Patient!"*

God, if I heard him say that one more time I was going to destroy his house!

Finally on Friday, Winston returned from his business trip. He never told me what the trip was for and I didn't really care. He did tell me that he had arranged to have a conference call with the leader of the Metis group in Edmonton next week and that he was pretty sure it would come through.

At last! A glimmer of hope! I was almost giddy at the thought of having something meaningful to do again! The conference call couldn't be arranged until the following Wednesday, so I spent another two useless days sitting in Winston's kitchen listening to his business dealings and waiting for the conference call.

Finally it happened. I sat at Winston's kitchen table and listened to him introduce me on a speaker phone to a man named Shane who was the president of a Metis Nation group that had a potential assignment available for both me and Yolande to work on. I spoke to him for about 2 minutes and then he took over, jabbering non-stop about how he had a number of economic opportunities that he needed help creating business plans for. He talked so fast and went in so many directions at once that I had a hard time understanding exactly what the opportunities were that he was talking about, but he definitely sounded excited and as long as he had *something* for me and Yo to do, I was excited to. We ended the call by arranging for Winston, Yo and me to meet him and his partner next week in Grand Prairie, a city about 3 hours away from us.

I wasn't sure exactly what kind of business plans he was looking for since I never really prepared any during my days as a corporate accountant, but Winston assured me that he had plenty that I could use as models and that it wouldn't be difficult for me to do, once I had all the facts and figures I needed. I was pretty sure I could handle it also, but even if I had any doubts, Yo and I were ready to get out of Coyote Lake and get started on a new assignment, whatever it was.

It took another week, but finally the big day came when Winston, Yolande and I would drive to Grand Prairie to meet Shane and his partner from the Metis Nation group. I did the driving because Winston had been unable to renew his driver's registration and didn't want to risk getting a traffic ticket if he drove on an open highway. During the three hour drive, Winston talked at length about his experiences growing up in the reservations schools, how he had run away from them several times and how many of his boyhood friends ended up committing suicide as a result of the harsh treatment they had to endure.

Despite all the problems we had encountered, I had developed an admiration for Winston's will to survive and the way he had overcome all the obstacles he had experienced. During this trip, however, he mentioned his wife's brother who was a partner for a large law firm in Vancouver, and the fact that her family had vast parcels of real estate in New Brunswick. I began to suspect that part of his financial success had a lot to do with his being married to Donna. He definitely didn't seem very well organized for a top businessman. However, at this point I didn't really care about his disorganization as long as he could finally find something worthwhile for me and Yolande to do, and get us out of Coyote Lake.

We got to Grand Prairie and found the hotel where we were supposed to meet Shane and his partner Darren. We walked in to the hotel lounge where they were sitting at a table drinking a few beers.

They both looked to be in their early forties, Shane being slim with light brown hair and Darren being tall, dark and hefty. Neither one of them looked like they had any Aboriginal blood in them, but we sat down to discuss how Yo and I could be of some help to their organization. Winston gave them the basic information about who we were and how we had volunteered to work with the foundation which specialized in helping First Nations organizations in Canada and how we had been left high and dry by the Wild Hawk band in Coyote Lake. Shane and Darren listened attentively, asking a few questions here and there, and then Shane began his presentation about what he wanted me and Yo for.

Winston, Yo and I sat and listened to what can only be described as one of the most ego-centric, non-stop, self-congratulating speeches I had ever witnessed. This guy was either the greatest fund raising genius that ever lived, or he was just the most egotistical. According to Shane, he had investors just begging him to pour their money into his projects and Aboriginal owned businesses. He knew where to find millions, not thousands, but *millions* of dollars for his projects, and made it clear that he didn't need any help from Winston or anyone else in securing funding. What he wanted was someone to do the paperwork to secure the grants and investments he had waiting in the wings. This is where Yo and I came in.

Shane's idea was to have someone like me, who had a business background, and could gather all the basic information he would provide for some of his proposed projects and turn it into a first class investment proposal to send to his eager investors while at the same time comply with the government regulations related to First Nation or Metis organizations. All of this sounded fine, of course, but he didn't stop there. He went on and on about how he was such a talented money man and how his organization was about to grow so fast he wasn't sure he could keep it all under control. He definitely wanted us to know that he was God's gift to the Metis Nation groups in and around Edmonton and expected all of us to be duly impressed.

We did our best to look that way, but after the first ten minutes or so, we all just wanted the meeting to come to a merciful end.

Still, he was agreeing to use me and Yo as volunteers to get his business plans off the ground and to pay all our living expenses, just as the Wild Hawk had done. This sounded good, too, and Shane ended his lecture by telling us to meet him at his office in Edmonton the following Tuesday, which was the day after the Canadian Thanksgiving holiday.

We were definitely grateful to finally have a new assignment, but as we all drove back to Coyote Lake, I reminded Winston once again that I still had not received the reimbursement checks that Tyson had promised would be paid to me the week before. Winston promised to take care of it the very next day.

The next day at Winston's house, I asked Winston if he had talked to Tyson about our expense reimbursements yet. He said no, he hadn't had the time, but I could just walk over to the band office and speak to Chief Tyson about it myself and that would probably work just as well.

Right, Winston. Thanks for all your help in getting this resolved- *again!*

I called Tyson on the phone and was surprised that he actually answered right away. I asked him about the status of the payments and he said "Oh, yeah! I've got it right here! Someone had left it with the receptionist and thought you were coming in to get it! You can come over right now, if you like." I told him that would be fine, and I walked over to the band office building, muttering to myself about how useless Winston was when it came to following through on anything. Before I got to the entrance, I heard Tyson call out my name.

"Hey, Mike!" he called out. "I've got your check!"

I walked over to take the envelope form his hand. To my amazement, the envelope held not just one check, but two! I looked at the amounts involved and realized what had happened. The band had obviously made out a separate check for our travel expenses from the Canadian border to Coyote Lake and then also included those expenses in the second check with all our other costs incurred for the first four weeks.

"Is that right?" he asked.

"I think so," I said. I'll check it against the spreadsheets.

"Fine!" he said and shook my hand. It was a handshake that seemed to say "Okay, you got what you wanted, now get out of here and leave us alone!"

I knew the two checks were more than the band planned on paying me, but I still had another three weeks of expenses that they hadn't paid yet, so I figured I would just deduct the second payment from the final unpaid expenses.

I came back to Winston's house and told him that I finally got part of the payments due to us. He congratulated me and then sprang one more surprise on me. He had two more volunteers from England arriving at the Grand Prairie airport the next day and wanted to know if I could drive! He still didn't have his registration renewed, so he still couldn't drive on the highways! Of course, I had nothing else to do until we left for Edmonton, so I said sure.

We picked up Beth and Geoff, the young couple from England at the airport the next day and on the drive back I listened to Winston explain how the foundation provided benefits to the First Nations groups and how they would be working for another band in Running Bison, the next town over from Coyote Lake. Winston would introduce them to the chief of the band within the next two days and they would begin their assignments the following week. It all sounded good, and I sincerely hoped that it would work out that way, but by now I took everything Winston promised with a grain of salt. We then drove back to Winston's house where Yo and Donna joined us for a final farewell dinner.

On our last day in Coyote Lake, Yo and I worked on reorganizing the school library which had almost no filing system for any of their books until Yolande began working on it during the last week there. During our time there, the other teachers at the school had become very friendly with Yo and they were all a little sad to see her go. As we finished the library project they all came in along with the school principal to present Yo with a gift card as a going away present for all her help. Then we went back to Winston's house to say goodbye to him as well as Geoff and Beth before leaving for Edmonton in two days. Winston and Donna also gave us a card with a going away present and wished us well. Even though I was never impressed with Winston's attention to detail and follow through, I had to admit they had both been pretty good friends for the month and a half we were there.

We went back to the house in Peace River and got everything packed and loaded up into our Toyota one more time for the five hour trip down to Edmonton. We weren't really sure if we would enjoy working with Shane and his group any more than we did with the Wild Hawk band, but at this point we really had no choice. So we crossed our fingers and headed south, hoping that *this* time we'd finally be able to do something worthwhile for the Aboriginal or Metis Nation peoples and that our days of fighting for our expense reimbursements and my days of endless, frustrating boredom were over.

But you know what they say: *"The grass is always greener on the other side of the fence."*

Greener or not, we were headed to Edmonton.

****

Edmonton Episode

*"Got to pay your dues if you want to sing
the blues
And you know it don't come easy!"*

-Richard Starkey
It Don't Come Easy

We got to Edmonton on the Sunday before the Canadian Thanksgiving, which fell on a Monday in October. I never knew why the Canadians celebrated Thanksgiving a month before the Americans, and why it came on a Monday instead of a Thursday, but that's the way they did it. We definitely didn't mind, since it gave us a day to explore the city and a regional park famous for its buffalo herds before we settled down to work with the Metis Nation group.

We were staying at a motel on the west side of the city, which was about a 45 minute drive from Shane's office in Sherwood Park. We found a motel that wasn't too expensive so there wouldn't be any problems with getting reimbursed for the cost. The foundation had promised us free lodging in return for our volunteer work, so this would be included in our reimbursements.

Originally, Winston had told me to find a reasonably priced apartment near the office where we would be working. I spent the better part of a day searching the internet for apartments for rent in the Sherwood Park area. I showed the list to Winston and his only comment was "That's way too expensive. See if you can find anything cheaper." I did find a few apartments that were cheaper, but they were also further away from the office. Since Winston said I should find something within a half hour commute, this was turning into a real challenge.

Also, I didn't know how Yo and I were supposed to rent an apartment without a full time paying job, being from outside of the country AND only wanting a 9 month term. I tried to discuss this with Winston, but he was always too busy checking his emails or talking to one of his business partners on the phone. When I finally narrowed the search down to 3 possibilities that fit Winston's criteria, I asked him how he would arrange having the foundation pay the monthly rent while Yo and I were there. As usual, he simply brushed it off with his standard "I'll take care of it" line. When it got to be the Friday before we were ready to leave Coyote Lake, I asked Winston if he had contacted the property manager for any of the three properties. He said he hadn't, but not to worry, just pick one of the apartments and rent it in the foundation's name.

Rent it in the foundation's name? How was I supposed to do that? I thought to myself.

I didn't know how things worked in Canada, but in the U.S. I knew you had to be an officer of a corporation or charity to rent property in the business' name. I asked Winston whose name I should put down as the lessor, since it would have to be an officer of the foundation if the apartment was to be rented in the foundation's name. He thought about this for a few minutes and finally said, "I'll have to call somebody and find out. In the meantime, just rent a motel room for the first week and I'll get the information so we can get it all taken care of when I get down there."

I knew right then and there that there was no way in hell I could rent an apartment in the foundation's name without being an officer of the foundation, and if Winston knew of a way to do it, I wanted to see how. He talked about calling up Dave Evans, the foundation recruiter that Yo and I contacted initially and seeing if we could fax a lease agreement to him for his signature. Somehow I didn't think that would fly either, and sure enough, after he spoke to Dave it was a "no go".

I couldn't figure out how such a successful businessman as Winston could not understand the basic mechanics of renting an apartment. I could not see any way anyone would rent us a property knowing that we would not be paying the rent directly and some foundation that they probably never heard of would be paying by bank transfer each month. In addition, all I had to show for my connection to the foundation was the contract letter they had sent me which didn't mention anything about renting a property in the foundation's name.

The whole thing was so crazy I started thinking that Winston might not be the successful businessman that I thought he was after all. He was very likeable and genuinely interested in helping First Nations people, but he didn't seem to understand basic business concepts. Either that or he was so wrapped up in his own business dealings that he didn't really pay attention to anything else. Either way, I knew it would be a problem if we actually had to find a place other than a local motel.

However our biggest problem came to light when we returned to our motel after the first day of sightseeing around Edmonton. Yo called her mother in Holland and found out that the ALS disease she had been diagnosed with about 6 months earlier had progressed significantly faster than expected. So fast, in fact, that she basically wanted Yo to come to Holland to live with her and take care of her until the time came when professional care was needed.

We knew, even before leaving California that we might not be able to finish out the entire 10 month assignment, however. Three days before we left, Yo's mother called and told her she might be needing full time help soon. We had literally just finished packing our car and were on our way to stay with our friends in Playa del Rey for a few days until we received our Canadian visas when she dropped the bomb.

Yo told her we couldn't possibly change our plans right then as we had committed to a 10 month project as volunteers for the First Nations charity, and they were expecting us there any day. Yo's mother said she understood, but warned her that she might need her to return to Holland a lot sooner that she originally expected. Yo told her she would come when her mother's muscle control declined to the point where she needed someone besides Yo's 85 year old father to take care of her. That seemed satisfactory, and we left for Canada thinking that we might have to terminate our volunteer assignment in about 6 months or so if she got much worse.

Now we had been in Canada less than 2 months since that first call, and it appeared that the assignment would actually get cut much shorter than that. Yo agreed to return to California in one week to gather some household goods and clothes that she would need and then return to Holland to help her mom.

Obviously this meant we would have to inform Winston and Shane, on the very first day we came to work in Shane's office in Edmonton, that Yo would have to leave after just one week. We gave them the bad news after our initial welcome luncheon on the day after Thanksgiving Day.

Shane and Winston took the news very somberly and didn't say much at first. Then they basically said they would be sorry to lose her so quickly, but if her mom needed her to help care for her, they understood why it had to happen. I would stay behind to help get the business plans and proposals for the Metis Nation projects started, but I told them I too would be leaving no later than mid-December.

None of this was exactly good news for Winston, Shane and Darren, who had all gathered in the small office's conference room for a "game plan" meeting to prioritize the projects Shane had ready for us to start on. They were obviously not pleased, but due to the nature of Yo's imminent departure, they couldn't really say too much about it. In any event, we spent the rest of the afternoon "prioritizing" various projects which Shane wanted to get underway.

I didn't think the assignments waiting for me would be too difficult, especially with Winston's help, since he had supposedly created hundreds of proposals and business plans for projects similar to this. However, at the end of the afternoon, Winston told me he would not be staying in Edmonton to assist with the myriad of projects Shane had laid out for us. He was going back to Coyote Lake. That night.

So much for getting some assistance from my "mentor", I thought. Winston was leaving me high and dry to figure out what I had to do on my own.

The good news was he promised to send me a template via email that I could use to prepare any of the projects Shane gave me to work on. I understood the basic overall concepts and knew that Yo and I would simply have to work on mining data from several internet sources to get the detail and statistics needed to flesh out the narrative. I still didn't appreciate Winston's quick exit, but by this time I was getting used to his superficial lip service, so I figured I would just have to muddle through without him.

During the next three days, Yo and I scoured the internet for articles and information related to the project we were preparing a business plan for. Although she hated the idea of being stuck in an office all day, she came up with quite a bit of good information which I could weave into the text of the business plan. In between our research activities, Shane would drop in to treat us to a 20 minute monologue which was apparently designed to impress us with how great a fund raiser he was. The bottom line was it didn't add anything to what we were trying to accomplish, but since he was the one theoretically funding *us*, we tried to at least appear interested.

On Friday, three days before Yo was scheduled to fly back to Holland, Winston called to tell us that he had found housing for us. It was slightly less expensive than the motel, and it was a little closer to the office, but it was still just a temporary solution. We would be renting a room in a private home owned by a friend of Winston's cousin, who lived in Edmonton. I told him that was fine with us, so he gave me the phone number of a woman named Jeannie. He told me that he had talked to her and arranged for us to stay there until he could find a way to rent a "permanent" apartment. All we had to do was call her and make arrangements to move in the next Sunday. I called Jeannie that afternoon and set up a time for Yo and I to move in late Sunday afternoon.

Sunday morning we moved out of our motel, loaded up the Toyota once more and did a little more sightseeing around Edmonton. We drove through the downtown area and got out and walked along a riverfront park taking a few pictures, enjoying our last day together for a while. The next day Yo would be leaving for Holland and I would be joining her by mid-December at the latest. By that time the foundation thought they could have two more volunteers arrive from Australia to take our place. The day was cloudy and overcast, kind of matching the gloom we felt regarding our pending separation. Finally at around 5:30 that afternoon we headed to the address we had been given to move into my new temporary quarters – and Yo's for that one night before she left for the airport in the morning.

We drove to the house at the address we had and saw no lights on inside. I walked up the steps to the front door and knocked. No one answered so I tried again, and another two times after that. We drove around the area for about 20 minutes before we returned to see if anyone was home now.

The house was just as dark as before, but this time there was an SUV parked directly in front of it with the engine running. I parked in the space a few feet in front of it and started walking back to the front steps. As I passed the SUV I could see a hefty looking black man sitting in the driver's seat chatting away on his phone. I wondered if he could possibly be coming to rent a room too, but he didn't seem to notice me as I walked by. I continued to the door.

As I started to walk up the front steps, I heard someone behind me yell out in what sounded like a Jamaican accent "There ain't nobody home now, mon!"

I turned around to see who was doing the yelling. It was the man in the SUV. I walked over to the driver's side as he rolled down the window.

"Are you here about the room, too?" I asked

The big man laughed and said "No, mon, I live here!"

I was a bit confused.

"Oh," I said. " I got this address from someone who said there was a room we could rent."

"Yeah, I know, mon! That was Jeannie! She's supposed to be here now, but she is late!"

"Oh, you know Jeannie?" I asked.

The man laughed at this also. "Yeah, I know her, mon! She's my wife!"

Okay, this was getting a little strange again. The woman I talked to on the phone definitely didn't have anything close to a Jamaican accent, and since Winston told me she was a friend of his cousin, I assumed she was also an Aboriginal or First Nations person. But for some reason I never pictured her as being married to a Jamaican in Edmonton, Canada, of all places.

However, my only concern at this point was if we actually had a room to stay in.

"Do you know when Jeannie will be here?" I asked.

"Don't worry, mon! I'll let you in! I just have to finish talking to my buddy on the phone!"

Okay, I thought, I guess we'll wait. I walked back to the car where Yolande was waiting and got in.

"Who was that?" she asked.

"Apparently he's our landlord," I told her.

"*Him???*"

I could see she was as surprised as I was. Not that we cared who we would be staying with, as long as they were honest and friendly, and since they had been recommended by Winston, we had no reason think they wouldn't be. But we honestly never expected to be living with an obese Jamaican man in Edmonton, Canada.

After another 5 or 6 minutes the big black man finished his call and slowly got out of the SUV. Yolande and I got out of our car and walked back to meet him. As he exited the SUV we saw that he was so extremely overweight that he could barely get out of the car and stand under his own power. Once he did he was already panting from the effort. Nevertheless, he stuck out his hand and introduced himself.

"I'm Glenn", he said.

Yo and I introduced ourselves and started following him up the front steps to the house. Each step seemed to take tremendous effort and he would have to stop to catch his breath with every step climbed. There were only 8 or 9 of them altogether leading up the slope of the front lawn to the small white clapboard house, but after each step he had to stop to regain his balance, and I was afraid he might actually fall backwards on us a couple of times.

When he finally made it to the top step he stopped to catch his breath and wipe his brow. "Wow!" he gasped. "I *hate* those steps!" I assumed I would probably hate them too if I had about 350 pounds to carry up on them. As he unlocked the door another car drove up on the street and parked behind the SUV.

A pretty black woman in her early 40s got out of the car with a shopping bag full of merchandise.

"Jeannie?" I asked.

"Yes, hello, Michael! Sorry I'm late!"

We finished our introductions inside the house. She introduced us to the large black man saying, "This is my husband, Glenn!" to which he replied "Yeah, mon! We already met! You are late!"

"I know," she said. "I'm sorry, I got stuck at work."

I asked her what kind of work she did. She told me that she actually had three jobs: one that she worked on 3 or 4 mornings per week as an intake nurse at a clinic, where she worked with Winston's cousin, one that she worked 3 or 4 evenings per week as a clerk at a retail store, and another job on weekends doing something else. Clearly, this was not a woman who was taking life easy in the Great White North.

We went inside to look at the room. It was simply a spare bedroom with a large, king size bed and a dresser, closet and bookshelf with all manner of knick knacks and odds and ends. One good thing about it was that it also had a large flat screen TV included which I looked forward to watching some football games from the States on. During the orientation she explained that she had to work 3 jobs because Glenn was disabled (or some might say, extremely obese) and could only get occasional work doing whatever he did. In addition, they had a grown son who worked as an electrician and lived in a room in their basement. He didn't come home until late and always left very early in the morning, she told me, so I probably wouldn't see much of him, if at all.

It appeared that the house wasn't really large enough for the three people who lived there because the living room, which was just off the hallway entered through the front door had shopping bags filled with merchandise and groceries sitting all around on the floor, and there were also piles of clothes on a sofa and a couple of chairs. It seemed like an odd way to store your purchases to me, but then it might just be temporary, and hey, what did I care as long as they had a room available at the agreed upon price?

It was definitely a step down from the spacious quarters we had enjoyed living in at Chief Tyson's house in Peace River, but it was definitely livable. Also, even though we had to pay $250 per week to live there, it was still less than what we were paying at the motel, and it was all part of the expenses that the foundation or the Metis nation would eventually have to reimburse us for, so it was totally acceptable.

Everything seemed fine until Jeannie told us about the shower. The only working shower in the house was down in the laundry room in the basement. It wasn't enough for us to reject the whole deal, but at the same time, I wasn't crazy about having to walk down the stairs in my underwear, in a stranger's house each morning to take a shower in a basement laundry room. I guess I'd been spoiled by never having to go to those lengths for my daily bathing up until then. But if it was only for a week or two at the most, I figured it would be alright. But even then, in the back of my mind I knew it would be longer than that. In any event, we had no practical alternative but to take the room as we had agreed to, so we handed over our cash and unloaded everything we needed for that night from the car.

The next day Yo flew back to California for a short sidetrack before returning to Holland and I returned to the office of the Metis Nation group. My task was basically to continue to work on crafting a business plan for a native interpretive center/museum that Shane had designated as the first project he needed done. Although Shane actually provided very little direction other than providing a sample plan that he had prepared for another project, by the middle of the week I was able to create a rough draft that I could send to Winston for his approval and suggestions.

True to form, Winston didn't respond to my emails until Thursday. The first draft of the business plan looked good, he said, just follow the format that he and Shane had provided. His comments were so vague, that I was pretty sure that he hadn't read it at all. Oh well, I thought, he's supposed to be the leader on this assignment, so if Shane and the Metis Group didn't like it, he would have to bear the brunt of the blame. However, he assured me that I was on the right track and I just had to add a few more statistics and illustrations and it would be ready to give to Shane.

Then he dropped a new bomb on me. Geoff and Beth, the English couple that we had picked up at the airport a few days before we left Coyote Lake, had run into problems starting on their assignment in Running Bison. It seems that the band there wasn't quite ready to give them any work to do and didn't even have any housing ready for them to move into. So ever since their arrival, they had been living in Winston's house, waiting to be given something to do.

Hmmmmm! For some reason, that sounded awfully familiar!

All of this further reinforced my opinion that Winston was really a piss poor manager. Now he had not only dragged me and Yo all the way up there to work on an assignment that would be terminated after only a month, he had also done it to poor Geoff and Beth, who came all the way from England to be misused.

But the real kicker was still to come. Now, Winston told me he would be driving down to Edmonton the next day to drop off Geoff and Beth to work as my assistants until he could find another assignment for them.

Assistants? I didn't need any assistants! I barely had enough to keep ME busy 6 or 7 hours per day! What was I supposed to have them do?

Oh, don't worry, Winston said. Just have them do some research on the internet for the projects you're working on.

Do some research? Yo and I already did almost all the research we needed! You said yourself that the first draft I sent you was good enough to submit to Shane! How much more research were we supposed to do?

By now, I was really getting sick at having to deal with Winston's incompetence. However, since I was already there and had committed to help work with the Metis Nation for at least another month, I didn't see that I had any practical alternative. When I asked Winston where they would be staying, he said not to worry about that because he had made arrangements for them to stay at his cousin's house. I wondered why it was Geoff and Beth who were staying at his cousin's house, when I was relegated to staying with a *friend* of his cousin in a house where I had to take my showers in the basement laundry room! On top of that, the house they were staying in was a half hour away from me in the opposite direction from the route to the office, and since they didn't have a car, I would be their designated driver to get them back and forth to the office each day.

I didn't know how anyone could be so incompetent as to have no back-up plan for either me and Yo or Geoff and Beth if our assignments didn't work out, but obviously planning ahead was not one of Winston's fortes. Now we had another mess to deal with, so I figured the best thing to do was to try to make the best of it. I tried to plan some assignments for them to work on with me, but when I left the office that day, I still wasn't sure what I could have them do.

The next day Winston, Geoff and Beth arrived. Winston stayed in the office for less than a half hour, just long enough to make some introductions to Shane's small office staff and then he claimed he had to go back to Coyote Lake or B.C. or someplace else to take care of some business. Geoff and Beth were overjoyed to be brought there because, as Geoff told me "We'll *finally* have something to do!"

He told me how disappointed they had been that they weren't actually able to work with the band in Running Bison, as they had been promised, and had nearly died of boredom from hanging around Winston's house all day for the last two weeks. I told them not to get their hopes up too high because the projects I was working on were a far cry from what I thought I would be doing for the foundation, and it was definitely not what anyone would consider exciting (or even mildly interesting.)

They said they understood, but they were still glad to be out of Winston's house and were ready to pitch in and help any way they could. I put together a list of topics related to First Nations culture and asked them to research them for possible use in the business plan. They gratefully took the list and started searching the internet for information. Although, it was definitely more of a "make work" project than anything, I was glad to at least have someone else to talk to and share complaints about Winston's ineptitude.

On the second morning that Geoff and Beth came with me to the Metis Nation group's office, Shane made one of his relatively rare appearances. Although in theory, he was supposed to be eager to get the business plan I was working on finished so that he could obtain the funding he said he had ready and available from his multitude of investors, he was hardly ever in the office. Any time I asked him a question about getting the details I needed to understand the timing and scope of the project, he would promise to send me more information later that day, or put me in touch with another business associate who could provide the information I wanted. Then he would either send an email with as little information as possible or tell me to just use whatever I had and we would fill in the missing pieces later. I got the impression that he basically wanted to spend as little time with me as possible, so that he could concentrate on his fund raising efforts. He was always after "a bigger fish", so after a while I didn't even expect to get anything useful from him and did my best to work around him and find what I needed from other sources whenever possible.

Therefore I was very surprised when he walked over to the table in the small lunchroom area that I had been working in for almost two weeks, and which now would be the workspace that Geoff, Beth and I would have to use, and introduced himself to the newcomers. I had already told them that Shane was a little "different" to say the least, and he didn't disappoint them with their first meeting.

After sitting down at the table, Shane looked directly at Geoff and Beth and said "Due to the time limits I have to work under, I'm going to force a dialogue right now!"

'Force a dialogue'? *Force a dialogue?* What the hell did that mean? It sounded like something the villain in a low budget action movie would say!

I can't honestly say that I remember exactly what he said after that, but it was pretty much one of his canned speeches that was designed to impress his audience with his amazing marketing and financing abilities. It consisted of about 5 full minutes of self-congratulatory rhetoric, and when it was finally over he paused for a few seconds as if he might be expecting applause. Geoff and Beth did their best to appear impressed but I knew they were probably thinking the same thing I was, namely "What the fuck is WITH this guy?"

Just before Shane started into his speech, Darren, his alleged business partner, walked over and stood slightly behind Shane's chair. Shane noticed Darren standing behind him out of the corner of his eye and had just started talking when he paused, turned his head slightly towards Darren and said "Are you just going to stand there or are you going to join us?"

Darren seemed a little surprised but mumbled "No, I'm just listening", as if he knew better than to interrupt the master.

After all was said and done, it really tuned out to be nothing more than a pep talk for all of us. I suppose Shane thought it was his duty to pump us up to try to get us enthused about having to spend long dreary days in a little office on the outskirts of Edmonton, trying to create compelling, professional business plans that would entice potential investors into pouring money into his projects.

After it was over and Shane ran off to one of his countless meetings, Geoff and Beth confided in me that they found his behavior just as bizarre as I did. But then, all of us had come to realize that our entire lives had turned into some type of bizarre, surrealistic existence.

There we were, all of us having left our homelands for the opportunity to work with disadvantaged people who had been relegated to living on government provided reservations in the hope of doing something to help them better their educational or economic lives. Instead we had arrived to find out that the housing that was supposed to be provided wasn't available, and the people we were supposed to be working with for the next 10 months or so, didn't want us there! On top of that, instead of being assigned to another group of native people that had a need for the services we had planned to provide, we were stuck in an office, preparing what was, in effect, something similar to a university level case study for a business opportunity loosely connected to a semi-Aboriginal group. To say we were a bit disappointed was putting it mildly.

On top of everything else, it appeared we would have a battle on our hands to get the expense reimbursements we were promised. I thought I had gotten this settled before I left Coyote Lake, but while Chief Tyson had finally succeeded in getting my expenses for the first four weeks there repaid, there were still three more weeks that had to be reimbursed, plus almost two weeks for the time that Yo and I had already spent in Edmonton. In addition, I soon found out that Geoff and Beth had never been paid for any of their expenses since arriving from England either. We all tried to be "good soldiers" and keep our complaints to a minimum, but the whole situation was starting to get close to being intolerable.

I spoke to Winston about this several times, and of course, each time I brought it up he gave me the now famous "I'll take care of it!" line. Now, however it seemed that there was an edge to his voice, so I tried to have some more patience and keep the faith a little longer.

After spending nearly two weeks putting the business plan together and trying my best to piece together two or three previous versions of the same plan created between 5 and 9 years earlier, I was able to corral Shane and show him the prior drafts that I was working from. I showed him the dates entered on the prior versions and how, based on some of his statements, it appeared that I was missing at least one or two versions. He spent all of 30 seconds looking at the documents and said "Yeah, you're missing the last draft that the Metis Nation of Canada did. I'll send you the phone number of our contact and you can have her send it to you."

Okay. I was under the impression that Shane wanted this project done as soon as possible, but now he sounded like he knew there was a missing piece to the puzzle and decided that I was far enough along now to get it.

When he sent me the phone number of the woman who was the apparent contact from the government organization I needed to talk to, she sounded surprised that I needed the document they had prepared. She asked me what I was going to use it for, and I told her that I was working as a volunteer to prepare a business plan for a "cultural interpretive center" for First Nation and Metis Nation people. Now she seemed doubly shocked and told me that *her agency was already working on a business plan for the very same project and were about halfway done!!!*

I told her that I was just as confused as she was and told her I would try to get more information from Shane. When I told him about my conversation with the government agency woman, he didn't seem at all surprised. He said he knew they had been working on it for some time, but in his mind, it was just one of many government related projects that the agency had to work on. He decided it would get done faster if he put me on it full time until I reached the point where I needed to meet with the agency people to see what they had done and then blend their data into my documents.

In any other type of environment, this would probably be considered strange. In most of the business organizations I had worked in, this kind of manipulation would have sparked an outrage at the lack of honesty involved. However, by this time I had become almost numb to Shane's bizarre behavior and at the total surrealistic aspect of how the entire volunteer experience had evolved.

Geoff, Beth and I spent the rest of the following week refining the business plan we had created, adding some last minute details and generally trying to make it as professional looking as possible. Shane had finally approved a meeting between us and the government agency people who were also working on the same project.

Our meeting was on the following Friday, so we made sure we had finished the document using as much information as we could find, and sent it to Shane's attention via email the day before, in case he wanted any final revisions. Of course, he was far too busy to review it, and told the three of us to just go to the meeting at the government agency's office and he would meet us there in the morning.

We drove to the agency's office that day and met the members of the team working on our business plan. Shane arrived about 15 minutes late and listened as the team leader reviewed the tasks that had been completed to date. One of the team members couldn't be present at the meeting, so he was attending via a conference call speaker phone. At one point, the speaker phone started squawking with static, and even though the man on the other end was discussing some fairly critical information related to financing the project, Shane interrupted him and told the team leader to turn the speaker phone off.

"It's too noisy and there's too much static," he said. "He'll just have to update the group with his information when he gets the final docs."

I didn't realize Shane was in charge of the meeting, but the team leader did what he told her to do.

After about a half hour or so, we presented the version of the business plan we had worked on to the group and waited for feedback. They were all very complimentary as they passed it around. Even Shane seemed pleased. I'm sure he wouldn't admit it, but I got the impression that that was the first time he had even looked at it.

The bottom line was we had completed the task were given to do, but again to my surprise, Shane told us later that day that we didn't have to work on that particular plan any more, even though there were still many gaps that needed to be filled in. We were going to let the government agency take it from there. He had other projects he wanted us to start on.

Our duties were now beginning to feel much more like a college class assignment than creating real life business plans. On top of that, as the following week wore on, it appeared that we would be getting less and less guidance from either Shane or Winston on any forthcoming projects. In addition, the research involved became even more vague and more boring. Shane asked me to update some spreadsheets he had created a couple of years earlier to present financial projections of the businesses supporting his Metis Nation projects. Although the spreadsheets were actually pretty complex and took me a few days to update according to Shane's instructions, Beth and Geoff were left with virtually nothing to do.

The thing which was now causing the most dissatisfaction among all 3 of us, however was the fact *that our damn expenses still hadn't been paid!* By now we had all just about run out of patience and decided it was time to call David, the recruiter who had been the first contact with the foundation for all 3 of us.

Winston had popped in the office for a visit during the prior week, officially to review our business plan doc, but in reality to drop off his truck at the windshield replacement shop in the same strip mall that Shane's office was located in. I actually had to drive him to the airport so he could take a plane to another one of his personal business meetings, and return for his truck a week or two later. During our drive to the airport, I once again reminded him that we *still* hadn't been reimbursed for our expenses, neither the ones that Yo and I had incurred in Edmonton, or the balance of the unpaid expenses from Coyote Lake, or *any* of Geoff and Beth's expenses.

Once again he said 'Don't worry! I told you I'd take care of it!"

This time I had an answer for him.

"Yeah, I know you'll take care of it, Winston! I'm just afraid I won't live long enough to see it happen!"

This stopped him for a moment, but only a moment.

"Okay, as soon as I get back I'll talk to Tyson about your expenses from Coyote Lake, and I'll send Shane an invoice so that he can pay the expenses due to you and Geoff and Beth for Edmonton tomorrow. You should have the money in your account by Monday. Tuesday at the latest!"

Guess what? Monday came and none of us got any money from anyone. Tuesday came and none of us had anything paid to us then either. I was tired of hearing Winston promise that he'd take care of it. Geoff and Beth were just about fed up with it too. It was time to call Dave at the foundation and raise hell.

We left the office and drove to a nearby McDonald's so we could use their WiFi to make a call to Vancouver on Skype. I knew that I might very easily get much louder than usual because by now I was totally frustrated at what a total debacle our assignments had become. We tried to find a spot away from anyone else so they wouldn't have to listen to my diatribe, but this was difficult to do because of the number of customers in the store around noon time. Oh, well, let 'em hear it all, I thought! I wasn't going to wait one more day without a definite payment date.

Poor Dave at the foundation could hardly have expected the tongue lashing he was in for. I knew it wasn't his fault, but I did feel that it was his responsibility. Even though it was Winston who had made all the false promises and screwed everything up, Dave was the official representative for the foundation, so he was the guy who had to fix it.

"Hello, Dave, I'm here with Geoff and Beth as well, at a McDonald's down the road from Shane's office."

"Hello, everyone," Dave said in his usual cheery voice. "What can I do for you?"

What followed was about five full minutes of me loudly telling Dave about all the mismanagement we had all endured, starting with the absence of lodging that we all experienced upon arrival at Coyote Lake, to the temporary housing we were living in now (including my basement laundry room shower situation) and culminating in our inability to get reimbursed for our expenses despite repeated requests to Winston. As I went on, my voice got louder and louder, despite my efforts to keep it under control and I ended by telling Dave that if we didn't get reimbursed as promised within the next few days, that I would personally go online to expose the foundation to let any other potential volunteers know how they would be treated. At one point, Beth even chimed in to let Dave know how Winston had essentially dumped both her and Geoff in my lap because he didn't have any place else to send them. This was 100 percent true, but I never wanted them to feel guilty about it. It wasn't their fault, after all, but I appreciated her telling Dave that she didn't think it was fair for Winston to simply expect me to become their chauffeur and supervisor without any advance notice.

Dave was understandably a bit shocked, not only from the problems he was just finding out about but also at the level of anger and frustration in my voice and also, to a lesser extent, in Beth's. After a long pause he let out a big breath and said "Well, I'm sorry to hear you've had so many problems. I know I had talked to Winston about expense reimbursements in the past, but he said he was taking care of it, so I assumed that's what he did."

I understood why Dave would think this. Winston was a highly respected businessman who had a Master degree in business, and had worked as a negotiator, consultant and financial advisor to several First Nations organizations and had recently been nominated to serve as the honorary president of the foundation. How he could be such a failure as a project manager was hard for all of us to understand. But, unfortunately, that was the case.

Dave basically tried to apologize to all of us and said he would be contacting Winston that afternoon and get the problem resolved once and for all. Geoff, Beth and I headed back to the office and I waited for the phone call from Winston.

It came around 3:30 that afternoon. I tried to ignore it at first, when I saw who was calling on my cell phone display. But then he called the office phone and one of the employees answered it.

"Michael, it's for you. Winston." He said.

I told him to let him know I would call him back in a few minutes.

I wasn't really sure how the conversation would go, so I tried to go into an empty office. I wasn't sure if Winston would be angry or not, but I didn't really care because I was definitely angry to have to go to these lengths to get our expenses paid as promised.

Winston answered the phone and said "Michael, I've been trying to call you. Dave Evans called me and told me about the conversation you had with him this afternoon. Why didn't you tell me you needed the money right away?"

At this point I basically exploded!

"I've been telling you I needed the money for the last 4 weeks! All you ever say in I'll take care of it, I'll take care of it, I'll take care of it! Well, I can't wait any longer! I don't have nearly as much money as you do, Winston!"

He seemed to be taken aback by this and replied, "Well, I don't have that much anymore!"

"Well, you've still got more than I do!" I told him.

"Listen, I'm sorry! I told Dave to send Shane an invoice and I thought he had already paid it by now and blah, blah, blah, bah, blah, blah…"

I told him I didn't care what the reasons were, I needed my money and Beth and Geoff needed their money too.

"Fine, fine, I'll send you a check out of my own account," he said. I would have sent it to you already if you had just told me you needed it!"

"HOW MANY TIMES WAS I SUPPOSED TO ASK YOU ABOUT IT?" Now I was really screaming.

Just then I heard a knock on the office door and Darren opened it cautiously to see who was in his office. I apologized to Darren and started to get up to leave, but he said there was no problem, he just didn't realize anyone was using it. (Right! He must have thought *I* thought he was deaf!) Anyway, Winston promised, *promised* that he would transfer the funds due to me, Beth and

Geoff for our expenses from Coyote Lake that evening, and he would have Shane issue a check for the expenses we incurred in Edmonton within the next week.

I went back to tell Geoff and Beth the good news. They were almost as relieved as I was, but I cautioned them not to celebrate until we actually had the money in hand. However, two days later, Winston had made good on his promise and we all went to the bank to withdraw the funds due to us.

The following Tuesday was Veterans Day, a fairly big national holiday in Canada. Darren told me as I was leaving on Friday, that many Canadians celebrated this holiday by making a four day weekend out of it. He mentioned that if we wanted to do so as well, it would not be a problem. When I told this to Beth and Geoff they were elated to be able to avoid two more long, boring days in the office. I couldn't blame them because even though I was still busy working on Shane's financial spreadsheets, they had practically nothing to do but aimlessly surf the net for "research" for future projects. I volunteered to be the driver if they found a place they wanted to visit during either of our days off and they took me up on it on Tuesday. We all took a trip to the Royal Alberta Museum and discussed whether or not it made sense for them to return to the office.

We all basically agreed that their usefulness had ended and even though their next assignment had not yet been finalized, Winston had actually made some arrangements for them to transfer to a teacher's assistance assignment at a school in the Northwest Territories. They still didn't know when it would happen, of course, but had been assured by Winston and Dave Evans that it would be within another week or so. That seemed like a good enough reason for them to stop coming to the office to assist me, so I told them they didn't have to come back.

I spent the next three days finalizing Shane's spread sheets and announced to him and Darren that I would have to leave for Holland sooner than planned because Yolande's mother was going downhill even faster than expected and she needed me to help her with her mom's care. This was mostly true. Her mother's health *was* slowly deteriorating, unfortunately, but it was not yet at the point where Yo would need me to assist her in taking care of her. However, like Geoff and Beth, I was not thrilled by the prospect of working in Shane's office any longer. I received little or no direction and was still missing the financial information needed to complete my assignment, which was promised but not provided.

Besides, I didn't need to be in the office to do any of it. Through the miracle of the internet, Shane could email me the spread sheet templates he wanted me to use and then provide the data or the people I had to contact to obtain the data to allow me to convert it into a business plan format. Surprisingly, when he heard that I would have to be leaving at the end of that week, he was the one who suggested I continue to work with him that way. He proposed a monthly retainer which he would pay me to allow me to continue to create whatever spreadsheets and reports he needed for his various projects, and he didn't care where I did them. As far as he was concerned I could do them anywhere in the world as long as I was able to get them completed by any deadline involved.

Of course, I was willing to do that and felt like I had misjudged Shane. Apparently he wasn't the arrogant egotist he seemed to be, but simply a sincere business person with poor "people skills". At least that's how I described him to Geoff and Beth when I met them for a farewell dinner the night before my last day at Shane's office. They were surprised and assumed they had misjudged him as well. We even included him in one of the many toasts we gave each other before we said goodbye. I told them I was sorry they got stuck in such a boring, mind numbing assignment, but they realized it was all a result of Winston's poor planning and thanked me for helping them with their reimbursements and also for a few sightseeing trips we took on the weekends. I was glad to be leaving but hoped they would be able to get transferred to their next assignment soon, too.

On my last day in Shane's office, I finalized all the spreadsheet reports I had been working on, made sure they were all named in accordance with his unique ID system and left him my email and contact information. He thanked me for all my efforts and told me he realized we had all been thrown into a strange environment (Wow! Even *he* knew it was strange!) and commended all of us for being professional enough to get the job done nonetheless. Best of all he gave me a check for all the remaining expenses I had incurred while in Edmonton up through that day and told me he would be sending me the reports he wanted me to work on while in Holland within the next week or so. I told him that I still hadn't gotten the contract he promised to send me to set up my monthly retainer and he apologized and told me he would have his bookkeeper send it to me via email first thing on Monday. Then we shook hands and I left the building.

I never heard from him or received any contact whatsoever from him again.

Looking back, it seems like the perfect ending to the most mismanaged assignment I ever had in my life. As I packed up my car early the next morning before starting the long drive back to California, I started thinking *"I should write a book about the things like this that have happened since I left the corporate world in America."*

And then, *"I wonder if anyone will believe it?"*

Return To Holland

"Many's the time I've been mistaken
And many times confused
Yes, and I've often felt forsaken
And certainly misused"

-Paul Simon
An American Tune

The drive back to California was one of the most beautiful routes I had ever driven. The road south from Edmonton to Calgary gradually meanders its way around to within a few miles of the Canadian Rockies, and the tricky part about driving this route is trying to keep your eyes on the road. The mountains were like beautiful white, snow covered sculptures rising out of the horizon to my right. I realized that this was basically the opposite side of the views we had seen in Banf and Jasper National Parks during our drive up on the western side. Now, with a blanket of snow around them, they were even more spectacular than what we saw back in August.

Further south, after crossing the border into Canada, the route continued through Montana, snaking its way around Great Falls,

Helena and Butte, where I stopped for the night. The Rockies on the American side were just as awe inspiring. My only regret was that Yo wasn't there with me to see the incredible scenery passing by.

The landscape continued to be amazing as I drove through southern Montana, then Idaho and into Utah. The hours went by quickly, as I had good weather for the entire trip and the road conditions were fine. When I got within 5 miles of Las Vegas in Nevada, I stopped at a fast food restaurant for lunch and used their wi-fi to call my old boss at the law firm in Los Angeles.

Dean had agreed to hire me on as a temp to help him with an accounting project for a week that would provide a welcome addition to my cash reserves. In fact, I later determined that working at the law firm for a week would almost pay for my trip from L.A. to Holland. Dean informed me of the parking arrangements and other details I needed to know to return to the corporate world one more time. I thanked him for providing this godsend to me once again, and then hit the road again for L.A.

I stayed at our friends' apartment in Playa Vista, a small secluded part of L.A. just south of Marina Del Rey. This was the same place Yo and I had stayed for 2 nights before we left for Canada, and where Yo stayed for a week before returning to Holland. Our great friends, Eddie and Natasha, were kind enough to once more share their home with me while I worked at the law firm in downtown L.A. for the week. While there, I visited our storage unit and packed up everything that had to be shipped to Holland. Everything else got donated to a local thrift store.

I had contacted my cousin Jenny and her husband Tony from the suburbs of Chicago about storing my car at their family's garage while we were in Holland. By another stroke of luck, they had space available and would let me store it there for free for the year or so I expected to be gone. I planned on hitting the road to drive to Chicago the day before Thanksgiving, but Eddie and Natasha insisted I stay to enjoy a Thanksgiving dinner with them and their friends. I knew I didn't really deserve having such great friends and relatives, but I always said I'd rather be lucky than good. I stayed for a delicious feast, enjoyed having conversations and a few games of poker with their friends, and set out on the road again that evening.

So after driving about 1700 miles from Edmonton to L.A. the week before, I was now back on the highway on a 2000 mile trip to the Chicago suburbs. It took almost the same length of time as driving down from Canada, although with the exceptions of Utah and parts of Colorado, the scenery wasn't nearly as remarkable. After arriving in the Chicago area, I met up with a few of my old high school buddies before dropping off my car to be stored in Jenny and Tony's garage. Tony dropped me off at the airport that evening and I was finally on my way back to Holland to reconnect with Yo.

I had mixed feelings about returning to Holland. It had been almost 3 years since I had been there, but I remembered the feeling of being an outsider from my last visit. Yo's family was cordial, but with a few exceptions, not exactly what I would call outgoing or welcoming. To some extent, this was because I didn't speak Dutch and couldn't join in on many conversations (although they all spoke English but seemed to prefer speaking Dutch). But in addition, I never felt like Yo's sisters were particularly fond of me, whether it was because I was an American or because of some other reason, I couldn't tell. All I knew was none of them seemed particularly interested in talking to me in any language and almost seemed to avoid any communication with me, from my point of view.

Of course, Yolande felt this was all in my head and that I simply need to be more outgoing myself to trigger better interactions. I'm sure this was true up to a point as well, but I found it somewhat awkward to try to begin conversations in English, or interrupt when everyone else was speaking Dutch. In any event, I hoped that the fact that Yolande and I had returned to try to help her mother through a difficult time with her illness might make our inter-relationships a bit friendlier this time around.

The other reason I was somewhat less than thrilled to be making a return visit was, of course, the reason why we were returning at all. Yo's mother's health was slowly deteriorating and her ability to do anything on her own had somewhat vanished by the time I arrived in early December. Upon entering Yo's parent' home, I saw her mother seated in a wheelchair at the dining room table. Yolande or someone else was saying something in Dutch that seemed to hold her attention for a few moments. Finally, after a break in the conversation, I walked over to her and put my hand on her shoulder.

"I'm so, so sorry for your problem," I told her. I knew she spoke some English but didn't know how much she would understand, so I tried to keep it simple. "I'm so, so sorry you have this."

Before I could say anything else, she dropped her head and began to cry. I stood there for a few minutes repeating the same line over and over, simply because I didn't know what else to say. After a short time Yo came over to talk to her and try to comfort her. I realized then that it really shouldn't matter how anyone else in the family treated me. The reason I was there was to be with Yo and to try to help her take care of her mom during the last few months of her terrible illness. Nothing else should really matter.

Of course, this was more easily said than done. As the days passed by, our routine became pretty, well, routine. Yo and her dad would try to help her mother eat by spoon feeding her at meal times, take her to the bathroom when nature called and talk to her and fetch things for her the rest of the time. I would only get pressed into service if Yo's dad was unavailable for any reason. At first I thought that she might be embarrassed to have me present when she had to be taken to the toilet, etc., but I soon realized that the only person who was embarrassed was me. Even though we hadn't ever been close, at this point all she cared about was having someone help her with her basic daily functions – eating, getting dressed, sleeping and yes, going to the bathroom. I realized that if I were in her shoes, I would probably want to be able to do exactly the same things, and I probably wouldn't care who it was that helped me.

In any event, as one day passed into another, our lives became absorbed into revolving around Rieke's needs. This was exactly what we were there for, so no one complained, but the monotony started to get to both me and Yo relatively quickly.

Yo and her dad (and I, on occasion) were expected to handle all the caretaking duties for her mother, including cooking and buying groceries, from Monday through Friday of each week. On the weekends, Yo's brother or one of her sisters were supposed to take over. Therefore, since the weekends were our only reprieve from the suffocating boredom we had to endure during the rest of the week, Yo made a point of finding an interesting get away spot for us to go to each Saturday and Sunday. When we returned I would usually post some of the pictures we had taken on our trip to Facebook on the internet. I'm sure all of our friends must have thought we were having a great life visiting castles and museums all around Holland and Germany, but the truth was it was the only thing we had to look forward to. So, needless to say, we rarely let a weekend pass without doing some type of short activity to help break up the week.

As the months slowly dragged on, it became obvious that Yo's mother would have to move to a full time care facility soon. When I got there, she had home care attendants coming to help take care of her 4 or 5 times per day, as well as having either Yo, her dad or me available to help her any other time, she needed more. On top of that, Yo and her mom did not always agree on what she had to have done, which led to several arguments and crying, often for reasons no one could understand.

By the time February rolled around, Yo and her siblings had come to the understanding that, because she needed almost constant attention, the time had come to search for a nursing home or full time care facility for her mom. It was a decision no one really wanted to make, but it was now obvious that it had to be done.

From a practical standpoint, Yo and I could not expect to continue living at her parents' house rent free and having our meals paid for if her mother would no longer be living at home and needing our help. So, since we couldn't come up with any practical alternative, we decided to once again seek foreign teacher or volunteer jobs in another country. We thought we had gone through a bizarre situation with Winston and the Wild Hawk band in Canada, but our search for foreign teaching jobs in the next few months would definitely make us feel like Alice through the looking glass.

Once we knew we would not be staying in Holland indefinitely, now that Yo's mother would move to a nursing home, I started searching the internet for foreign English teacher jobs. Although finding a foreign English teaching job would not be too difficult, the challenge involved would be to find a school or organization that would accept both Yo and me as teachers.

Many of the jobs for foreign English teachers require that an applicant be a "native English speaker" to be considered. This meant you had to have a valid passport from either the U.S., the U.K., Australia, New Zealand, Canada or South Africa. Even though Yolande had lived in the United States for almost 20 years and been speaking English since she was in high school, and had an advanced teaching degree on top of that, there were very few English teaching jobs she could qualify for because she was not a "native English speaker". However, we knew that we would eventually find some positions that she could be accepted for in a location that we both would not mind living in. The only question was how long it would take. When we posted our resumes on the internet before we landed our jobs in Chile, it only took 3 days. This time it would take quite a bit more time.

One of the positions we applied and both got accepted for was for a language school in southern Italy. We set up a time for a Skype interview from a small hotel room in France, while we were visiting a long lost cousin one weekend. The connection we had seemed very bad, as we got so much static after making a connection that it was impossible to hear anyone on the other side. The picture on my laptop was also vey fuzzy, but I could see a young, professional looking man in his mid -thirties wearing a shirt and tie and sitting at a desk. I tried to speak to him a couple of times, but the static made it impossible to communicate verbally. He sent a typed message saying that we should turn off the video and simply type our dialogue.

This seemed reasonable under the circumstances, and I certainly didn't want to miss an opportunity to go teach in sunny southern Italy for a year, so I complied. I then received a series of questions typed onto the Skype message box and I answered by typing as quickly as I could. After about a half hour, it seemed that the interviewer, a Mr. Colin, was satisfied with my answers and I had asked all the questions I needed to know right then. We ended our meeting after he indicated he would be in touch by email to let us know the next step we needed to take.

Within a few days, I received a contract by email from the school, along with instructions about how to send money to them to arrange our flights. The message stated that we would be paid back once we arrived at the school, but something about this arrangement made me suspicious. This was the first time any of the schools or organizations we had dealt with before ever requested any money in advance, for any reason. Plus, once this thought popped into my head, I took a closer look at the images on the contract itself. Instead of clear, distinctive logos and lettering, the seals and heading with the school name on it appeared faded, as if perhaps it had been copied from another document. Then I started looking more closely at the wording and found that there were several misspellings and/or incorrect grammar or tenses used in the contract.

This seemed extremely odd for a language school. However I knew from our experiences in Chile and China that foreign entities, even if they were legitimate language schools, did not always place much emphasis on spelling or grammar in their official correspondence. But then I was also wondering why every email I had sent to this school was only answered late at night, well after 10:00 pm in most cases, and why the Skype interview had been scheduled for a Saturday afternoon.

Yolande and I both had some questions to ask after reading the contract that was sent to us, so I sent an email back to Mr. Colin and the school, requesting an additional Skype interview. Once again, the reply did not come for 2 or 3 days and then it was once more very late at night. The reply asked us to send an email with all our questions so they could be answered that way, instead of via Skype. I insisted that we have a Skype meeting to discuss the details and the school reluctantly agreed to schedule another Skype meeting, also on a weekend, only this time late in the evening.

I contacted "Mr. Colin", or whoever was hosting the meeting on Skype at the appointed time. Once again, we experienced a lot of static that would make it impossible to talk to anyone. On top of that, before the video portion got disconnected, I could see Mr. Colin, once again – but he was seated at the same desk, wearing the same tie that he had during our first Skype meeting, and he didn't seem to be moving!

I typed in a few questions regarding the vacation policy, but grew even more leery when it took a few minutes before any answer was receive, and now I thought I could hear voices in the background over the static. The really strange part of this was that the voices sounded like they were speaking Russian!

By this time, I was sure that the whole business was just a scam, aimed at getting money from us in advance for our "airfares", or possibly also trying to get passport pictures and numbers to be scanned and sent to them for identity theft. I typed in a request for another phone number that I could call them back on a land line. The answer came back with a phone number I tried to call while still on the Skype screen and found out it was a fax number.

I typed in a request for a different phone number because the one they provided was for a fax. The answer provided was that I should use the same phone number that was listed on the school's website. I checked the official school website again and found that there wasn't any phone number listed. I typed this information and again asked for a working phone number that I could call back on. The reply that came back had the same fax number on it. Now I knew that this was a scam and decided to pull the plug.

I typed in a message saying I knew that whoever was typing the messages to me was not a legitimate language school and I knew they were conducting a scam. I told I was planning on reporting them to whatever authority I could contact to expose them and prosecute them if at all possible. The reply that came back was first a denial that they were conducting any type of scam, but it was quickly followed by a response of "Good luck!" They obviously weren't going to admit their true motivation, but I knew now that it was a total hoax. Both Yo and I were extremely disappointed, but we had no choice but to go back to the drawing board.

I applied to several different language schools advertising for foreign English teachers on the net, and eventually 2 or 3 replied with an invitation to have a Skype interview. One of the positions sounded very interesting, as it involved teaching at different locations in 3 different countries in eastern Europe. We were just about ready to accept this position when I received an email for a school in Ethiopia that I had applied to almost two months before. We scheduled a Skype interview, and to my surprise, both Yolande and I were offered jobs on the spot!

This was both good news and bad news because it meant that I would have to contact the owner of the school that taught lessons in the Czech Republic, Slovakia and Austria that I had previously made a verbal commitment to, and tell him I would have to back out of our tentative agreement. Understandably, he was not happy to hear this, especially since we had planned to meet in Prague that weekend to get me started on my first teaching assignment. However, the opportunity to work for an international school in Ethiopia sounded far too exciting for us to pass up. In addition, there was also no guarantee that both Yo and I would be able to teach every week for the school that I had tentatively given my acceptance to, so it seemed that we would have to turn it down now.

True to form, nothing we tried to do in regard to our foreign assignments ever ran smoothly. We spent the next 3 months sending emails back and forth and making phone calls to our recruiter, the principal of the school and its director in an effort to determine when were needed, what accommodations would be provided and how we had to apply for a legal working visa. All of this took at least 3 or 4 times longer than what one would normally assume because of the difficulty in maintaining communications with the school officials. Many times we would send emails to the principal, director and even our recruiter to get answers to specific questions, only to wait 4 or 5 days, and sometimes even 2 weeks to get a response.

Many times we were told after finally getting a reply back from one of the parties that the reason for the long delays were due to the sporadic internet access in Ethiopia. Other times, it seemed that the principals just didn't respond until I sent an email to tell them it was critical that we get some additional information if they wanted us to go there. Calling the principals was always a hit or miss affair also. Many times their cell phones were turned off for days or weeks at a time. Other times they simply didn't answer.

I had to resort to a variety of communications attempts in order to get any issues resolved. When trying to call the principals r send emails failed to elicit a response, I tried to call the school directly or send messages to their Facebook website to tell them I needed to talk with them as soon as possible.

After 2 months of going around in circles because of our communications problems I decided it was time to give up on the Ethiopian school. Then, just when I was ready to throw in the towel, I was able to call one of the phone numbers listed on their Facebook page and get through to the principal's brother, who was also the school's business manager. He seemed very pleased to hear from me and explained that his sister had been out of the country for a few weeks, which is why she hadn't answered any calls. He then told me he would be emailing a "letter" which detailed all of the specifics regarding the teaching positions. I hadn't expected any such letter, as our recruiter had told me that the school typically did not put all the benefits and/or duties in writing, but that the principal had agreed to our conditions per our initial conversations 2 months earlier. However, I'm a believer in trying to get as much in writing as possible, so I thanked him and asked when he would be sending it. As soon as we hang up, he said. Great, I said. I would be looking for it within a few minutes.

I ended the call and waited for his email. After 30 minutes, I sent my own email inquiring as to whether or not he would still be sending the letter. Almost 45 minutes later I got a reply. "Working on it," it said.

After about another hour or so, I got a new email from him. "I will send it to you tomorrow morning, after I edit it sometime around noon." Hey, after waiting almost 2 and ½ months to get everything resolved, what was another day?

The next day I got one more email right around noon, and sure enough, it had a letter attached with all the details regarding our compensation, housing arrangements and benefits. Unfortunately, the vacation benefit specified in his letter was not what we had been told it would be. Instead of 2 months' vacation during the summer after the end of one school year and before the start of another, the new benefit specifically stated that it would be only for 30 days.

I promptly sent an email back questioning if this was correct, and mentioning that we had plans to take care of personal business in America during the 2 months we thought we would have free. I asked if this meant we still would have 2 months off, but only one would be paid.

The return email stated that we would get one full month paid vacation but it also stated that we had to be available for half day summer school classes which overlapped with our stated vacation time. Now it seemed as though we would only have 2 weeks of paid vacation time!

This was a bit upsetting, to say the least, after we had spent so much time emailing and calling back and forth to try to get all the information needed before we made a commitment. I even had to call the nearest Ethiopian embassy in Brussels to determine what information they needed from the school to allow us to get our business visas. I then had to contact the school and ask them to contact the Ethiopian immigration department to get them to send a letter to the embassy. The school advised us twice that the authorization letters had been sent, but when I called the embassy to confirm this, they had not received them. Eventually they confirmed that the immigration authorizations had been received and we took the train to Brussels to fill out the paperwork needed.

It seemed like a classic bait and switch situation and once again I gave up on the possibility of teaching there. Yolande and I had even gotten vaccinations for 4 different diseases in preparation for the trip, but now it looked like it was ready to completely fall apart. We decided to follow through with interviews for a school in Santiago, Chile, which seemed very happy to have both of us come there to teach. We were disappointed that we wouldn't be going to Ethiopia, especially after all the time we had spent on trying to make it happen, but we enjoyed Santiago during our final vacation trip in Chile two years before, so it seemed like a reasonably attractive alternative.

We both had Skype interviews with the school in Santiago and were told we passed with flying colors. All systems were go as long as Yolande submitted a separate application with her resume and diploma attached. She just finished doing this on the morning that was the deadline for submitting applications for the next teaching assignment when we suddenly got a Skype call from the principal of the Ethiopian school.

"Alexis!" I said as I answered the call. "We've been trying to contact you for quite some time!"

I wanted to let her know that we were none too pleased to be kept hanging for so long, not knowing if they really wanted us to come there to teach. In addition, the drastic change in paid vacation time from our first conversations with the school's recruiter didn't sit too well with us either.

Alexis said she understood why we were concerned and apologized profusely for not being able to contact us sooner, but she swore that she had been in the U.K. on business for the past 4 weeks and for some reason was not able to get all my emails(!) This seemed a bit strange, given the fact that we had friends in the U.K. who never seemed to have any trouble receiving our emails or answering them on a timely basis. However, we decided to give her the benefit of the doubt and eventually worked out a compromise to salvage most of the vacation time we had been promised. Since both Yolande and I still wanted to experience teaching in Ethiopia, we decided to let bygones be bygones and agreed to arrive there one week later to begin teaching. After that we would take a 45 day vacation before returning to Addis Ababa and remaining there for the next 10 and ½ months. As it turned out we would be going to Ethiopia after all!

So now we finally had our next adventure scheduled and could start planning our lives again.

There was just one last problem to deal with: whether or not we would be able to stay until Yolande's mom decided it was time to put an end to her suffering and misery by taking advantage of Holland's euthanasia process.

Euthanasia, or "assisted suicide" as it is known in the United States, is completely legal in Holland, and in several other countries as well. There is a defined protocol that doctors and patients have to go through to insure that the patients are making the decision of their own free will, without any undue influence or pressure from anyone else. Yolande's mother, Rieke, finally decided enough was enough and decided to have a doctor give her the injection which would put an end to her problems in this world.

Her assisted suicide was scheduled to be performed 3 hours after we confirmed our assignment to Ethiopia.

****

Onward

"Nobody told me there'd be days like these!
Strange days indeed!"

-John Lennon
Nobody Told Me

It was definitely a bit ironic that Yo's mother picked the day she would die to be on the same day we got our notification that we would be going to Ethiopia after all. Yolande liked to think the reason we had to wait so long for the confirmation to come through was because God, or Fate or some cosmic force wanted us to stay in Holland until she died. I'm not sure if that had anything to do with it or not, but I'm not saying it didn't. In any event, she had already made her decision 3 days before we got our call, so she definitely wasn't waiting for us to give her the go ahead – not that she should have.

When I arrived in early December, Yo's mother was already in her wheelchair but could still speak fairly clearly and also still had partial use of her arms. By the end of March when she finally moved into a nursing home, she had lost the use of her limbs entirely, and now her speech was so slurred it had become extremely difficult to understand her. In between, we had about 4 months of escalating tension between Yo and her mother, which paralleled the gradual deterioration of her mom's motor skills. It was definitely not a pleasant situation, but it didn't come as a surprise. We pretty much knew what we were getting ourselves into. That's not to say we liked it, but it was basically something we felt we had to do.

One of the nights we spent at their house during this period was unusually dramatic. I woke up shortly after midnight and heard Yo's mother crying in her room across the hall. It also sounded like she was trying to call "Pa", her husband and Yolande's dad, who slept in a different room. Now, this might sound heartless, but by this time, Yo and I had been conditioned to try to not pay attention to things like this. Yo's mother had become increasingly depressed and emotional and often broke down into tears for reasons no one could understand. She also had a tendency to call "Pa" several times during the day and night to assist her with a variety of problems, some large, but many of them extremely small. Some might even say "petty". However, Yolande's dad was almost always the stoic good trooper who would march off to help her whatever the reason for her beckoning was, albeit in relatively slow motion.

This time, though, her plaintive calls seemed a bit different – a bit more urgent, almost desperate. I waited to hear Yolande's father rising from his bed in the next room and crossing the hallway to see what she needed. However, now I could hear Piet, her dad, asking her something in Dutch and slowly walking down the hallway towards the main dining room. I nudged Yo to ask her if she thought we should do something (which, in all honesty, was meant to be if "she" should do something, since I was pretty much useless if it involved anything that required talking to her in Dutch). Yo replied she didn't know, since she didn't know what was wrong. So we both got up from the mattresses we slept on in the spare bedroom and tried to switch on the light.

As soon as I tried to do this, I started to understand what the problem was. The electricity was off. If I was back in our apartment in Long Beach, I would know immediately what to do – just find the circuit box, flip the switches and restore the broken circuit. However, I had never even seen the circuit box in this house, and since I spoke very little Dutch, never really asked anything about the house or anything else, I had no idea where it would be. Piet would know, I thought and he had indeed shuffled down the hall to find the circuit box a few minutes earlier.

Still the cries from Yolande's mother's room persisted. "Pa!" she cried "Pa!" followed by something that sounded very desperate in Dutch followed by mournful crying. Now Pa was calling to Yolande and saying something in Dutch so we both walked into the living room to see what the problem was.

It seemed that Piet knew where the circuit box was but didn't seem to know how to reset any of the circuits in it!! Yolande was able to find a flashlight and eventually read the descriptions marked on each switch to try to find the circuit that needed restoration. Yo flipped a number of switches and was able to restore light in the living room area.

We still had not restored light in Yo's mother's bedroom however, and her cries became louder and more desperate. As if to provide some comic relief, Piet went into the living room which now had light and unplugged one of the lamps. He then took the lamp and started to carry it into Yo's mother's bedroom. I had to stop him in the hallway and try to explain to him in my best basic Dutch that taking a lamp from a working circuit and plugging it into a socket in a room in which there was no electricity wouldn't work. I don't think I convinced him, however, because he continued on his path with a look of determination on his face.

All during this time Yo's mother continued to wail and cry in her room. Eventually Yo found the right circuit switch and I flipped the switch to restore the light in Yo's mom's room. The crying and wailing finally tapered off and we eventually all got back to bed and went to sleep.

The next day I was sitting at the computer desk surfing the net, as always in an effort to find something to do and I noticed Rieke slowly pushing herself back from the table where she had been wheeled to eat breakfast (she was still able to use the wheelchair under her own power at this point). I could see her out of the corner of my eye slowly coming in my direction. This was a bit unusual because, although she had always been cordial and polite to me (at least to my face), we had so much difficulty communicating that, for the most part, we both stayed apart, for practical reasons. This time she slowly inched her way forward, so I knew she was determined to talk to me about something.

I turned to look directly at her to see what she wanted. She looked at me and started slowly saying something like "I am sorr-r-y for last ni-i-ight." I tried to tell her it was no big deal and not to worry about it, but I could see she wanted to tell me more.

She proceeded to tell me a long, drawn out story, which, because of how much her speech was slurred at this point, I could only understand bits and pieces of. I did hear her say something like "When I-I-I-I was in the camp in Indonise…", so I knew she was talking about her time in a Japanese prison camp in Indonesia during World War Two.

A bit of background may be needed here. Yolande's mother was born in Indonesia and lived there as a child while it was still a Dutch colony. She and her family were captured by the Japanese after the outbreak of the war, and she and her mother were subjected to some brutal treatment while they were imprisoned, including being raped before she was even in her teens. All my bad days put together couldn't match one of her worst days in that environment. As a result, although I never had much interaction with her, and she and Yo certainly didn't have the warmest mother – daughter relationship possible, I still respected Rieke for being able to survive the prison camp and eventually return to Holland to become a teacher and raise a family. Whatever faults she may have had, toughness and resilience certainly were not included in them.

As Rieke continued trying to tell me something in her slow, slurred speech, I heard her say something about an "oliedrum" or something like that, and I thought I had an idea that I knew what she was talking about. Yolande had told me that while her mom was in the prison camp as a girl, she did something that displeased her guards. As a result, she was forced into an oil drum and left in the hot sun for an extended length of time as her punishment. Hearing this story made me realize that an experience like that could certainly leave someone scarred for life. Now it seemed that Rieke was trying to tell me why she had reacted the way she did when all the electricity, including her night light went off the night before – she had been scared and it probably made her feel the way she did when she was confined to an oil drum in the prison camp!

As she continued talking to me, I could hear bits and pieces of enough words to confirm that this was probably what she was talking about. I don't know what else "Japanese", "Indonese" and "oliedrum" could have in common, or why she would be telling me about this in conjunction with apologizing for crying and wailing in the dark. I'm sure an experience like that might make anyone claustrophobic and afraid of the dark. Now here she was apologizing to me because she was afraid and this is what caused here to "make a scene" during the power failure.

Yolande and I had laughed about it the night before, mostly because of her dad's inability to find the circuit box and his idea to plug the lamp from the living room with electricity into Yo's mother's bedroom which didn't have it. But now I felt extremely guilty for ever finding anything humorous about her reaction to such a horrible experience.

Rieke finally wrapped up her long, drawn out apology and I could see it had left her with tears in her eyes. As usual, I couldn't find the right words to tell her how unnecessary it was to explain and she certainly had nothing to apologize for, so I just kept saying

"It's alright! No problem, don't worry! It's alright!" None of this seemed at all adequate, but she seemed like she had said what she wanted to say, so she slowly backed her wheelchair up and pushed herself back to the bedroom.

I watched her push herself down the hall and thought to myself that if the phrase "walk a mile in my shoes" ever seemed appropriate, this was certainly the best example I could think of.

****

Transition

"Do you get what you're hoping for?
When you look behind you, there's no
open door
What are you hoping for?
Do you know?"

-Michael Masser and Gerald Goffin
Do You Know Where You're Going To?

Rieke Wassenberg's assisted suicide was the first one I ever witnessed personally, and hopefully also the last. Not that it was anything horrible to watch, or anything like that – far from it. I just hope that nobody I know ever gets to the point where their bodies have become so useless to them, or so confining, and there is no hope that it will ever get better, that they would rather end their life than go on suffering and hoping for a miracle.

Such was the case for Yolande's mom. She survived the horrors of a Japanese prison camp in World War Two only to be betrayed and imprisoned again by her own body. Who could blame her for wanting to put an end to it after enduring almost an entire year of progressive deterioration and loss of muscle control? Not me, that's for sure. However, although I never doubted the necessity of her decision, I was somewhat surprised at my reaction to the execution.

The family gathered at the nursing home at a pre-arranged time, approximately one hour before the lethal injections would take place. Everyone was supposed to have a final luncheon together, which seemed a little superfluous to me and susceptible to comparisons to "The Last Supper". As it turned out, Yolande and I were late (because we were traveling by bike, as usual) and did not even participate in the luncheon. Obviously, that was not of any major concern to us anyway.

At approximately 1:00 p.m. the family rolled Rieke back to her room in her wheelchair to be bathed and dressed by two of Yolande's sisters in preparation for the doctor while the rest of us waited in what reminded me of a "green room" from my theater days. At approximately 1:45 we all gathered in Rieke's rom to say our final goodbyes.

One by one, each one of her children and her husband, Piet, came up to her and spoke to her, some calmly and soothingly, others more tearfully, but all of them lovingly. I held back, simply because I knew with my limited Dutch and her limited English that I probably wouldn't be able to say anything that would be meaningful or even comprehensible. Besides, I felt that this was something that should really be reserved for the immediate family and very close personal friends. Although I was married to one of her daughters, I never really felt that we had a deep personal connection with each other. Basically I felt it was best to let the people who meant the most to her have this time to themselves.

The procedure was actually a two-step process, although I didn't realize that at first. When we entered the room there was an EMT wearing a blue and yellow uniform searching in vain for an eligible vain in Rieke's leg or foot. He spent at least 20 minutes trying to find a suitable entry point for the first injection before he finally gave up and went searching for an assistant.

He came back with two other EMTs wearing similar uniforms who resumed the process but also failed to accomplish the task. Finally, an elderly doctor with a fringe of white hair on his head, wearing a dress shirt, wire-rimmed glasses and dress black jeans took over the operation and shifted the attack to finding a useable vain in her hand. After 15 minutes he finally succeeded and the lethal liquid slowly began dripping into Rieke's body. The whole process took almost another 15 minutes while the family spoke to her in soothing tones until the final batch of fluid which would ultimately finish the job was released.

Once the final injection was complete, the end came quickly. Rieke had stopped speaking or making any audible sounds even before this step took place and now looked completely at peace as the doctor confirmed that her heart had finally, mercifully stopped beating. The whole process went so calmly and smoothly that I somehow felt like it wasn't really happening while I watched it. It almost seemed like I was watching a documentary regarding end of life procedures. It may sound odd, but Rieke now looked so peaceful and serene, that it was difficult to believe she had actually just died right before my eyes. Somehow I thought it would be much more dramatic.

The family now had to wait for the coroner to come to prepare an official death certificate, and this seemed to take quite a bit of time. We all waited quietly, as the family chatted about happier times. After a suitable waiting period, one of the siblings decided it was appropriate to transfer Rieke's personal belongings out to their cars. Within an hour, everything had been removed. All that was left to do now was for the funeral home to pick up the body.

To my surprise, although I knew Rieke would be cremated, her body would not be taken to a funeral home to be waked, but instead would brought to her house – and kept right across the hall from the bedroom Yolande and I were sleeping in!

I have to admit, this threw me a little at first. I had never heard of anyone having a wake for their loved ones in their homes, although Yo told me this was not anything uncommon in Holland. Still, the thought of having a dead body lying across the hall from you for 4 or 5 days until the cremation ceremony took place seemed a little strange to me, to say the least. It wasn't that I had any fear or distaste at the thought of seeing Rieke's body lying on a bed in the room across from us every morning, I just really couldn't understand why anyone would want to have it done this way.

I told Yolande my concerns and she suggested that we could contact one of her friends and ask about staying with them, if it bothered me that much. I thought about this and actually considered it for a while. However, once the family arrived at the house, along with the funeral home people to set up the viewing room, I decided to just put up with it and see first-hand what it was like.

The funeral home people, a man and a woman, arrived at the house a couple of hours after us, all dressed in their formal grey uniforms. Before they brought Rieke into the house, they made a point of meeting everyone in the house, saying hello and introducing themselves. I shook both their hands when they came to me and tried to explain why any more conversation with me would be fruitless: "Hello, I am Michael, Yolande's husband and ik spreekt geen Nederlands!" They seemed to understand, and like most Dutch people, they actually spoke very fluent English, so it was really no problem at all.

They placed Rieke in a bed in her bedroom with a specially designed cooling system under the bed to keep the body from decomposing. I hadn't known about this piece of equipment before then, but this made the whole concept of an in-house wake a little more acceptable to me. Then, Yo's sisters took over decorating the room with flowers, pictures and memorabilia around Rieke's bed. The whole thing was actually very similar to most of the funeral home wakes I had been to in America. The only thing different was that you didn't get to go home and forget about it for a few hours. It was always there, every moment of the day until the burial or cremation took place.

I understood how the rest of the family felt that this was a more personal way to handle it, and supposedly Yo's mother requested that it be done this way too. However, from a practical standpoint and having had to plan both my parents' wakes and funerals, I felt it was a whole lot more practical to let the professionals take care of everything. But like it or not, this is the way it was going to be for the next 5 days and we would just have to make the best of it.

During the coming week, Yolande and her siblings greeted visitors who came to the house to view the body at all hours of the day and night. I stayed out of the proceedings simply because I couldn't speak Dutch and didn't know many of the people coming to pay their respects. On the few occasions when a friend of the family that I knew arrived, I did my best to join in the conversation and reminisce or commiserate with the visitors, as the situation required.

In the days before the cremation, the house was also abuzz with the siblings who were planning the formal ceremony. Not only did they have to have "invitations" printed to send out to friends and family, Yo's brother and sisters also prepared poems to be read, speeches to be recited and a Power Point presentation of photographs to be shown during the ceremony. The amount of time and effort they all put into these preparations made the funerals I had arranged for my parents years before seem utilitarian in comparison.

The ceremony itself took place on an uncharacteristically warm, sunny day. Although I had been somewhat skeptical about the extent of the preparations, and even irreverently joked to Yolande at one point that it seemed more like preparations for a Broadway play, I have to admit it came off very touching and dignified. I think that even Rieke, who was even more practical and unsentimental than either Yolande or me, would have been proud.

In the 2 days that followed the ceremony, Yolande and I busied ourselves getting clothes and supplies out of storage and packing for our trip to Ethiopia. The whole process of applying for the jobs, communicating with the school officials, making 2 trips to the Ethiopian embassy in Brussels to get our visas, getting the vaccinations required and working out the details of our employment agreement had taken over 3 months. At times, I had completely given up on the whole idea and tried to find worthwhile alternatives.

But Yo never doubted it would happen. She kept telling me that there was a reason all these things were happening. She believed that our plans to leave Holland and take other positions in other countries had fallen apart was because we were meant to stay in Holland longer. She felt that somehow we were meant to stay there until her mom decided it was time to die. Call it fate, God, a higher power or the cosmic order of the universe, Yo does not believe that anything happens by accident. In her mind, whatever happens is what is ultimately what was always meant to be. I'm not sure if I believe that everything happens this way, but I have to admit that, in this case, it did seem like there was something keeping us from leaving before Yolande's mom was ready to move on. So there may be something to it after all. I can't say I'm totally convinced yet, but I'm keeping an open mind - at least until I see how things turn out on our next journey! I've been wrong before, so who knows? All I can say is I never say "never"!

So now that all our family obligations were behind us, whether due to some type of cosmic force or otherwise, it was time to contemplate what to expect on our next adventure. In fact, it was time to stop and think about where we were going from here. I don't mean just in the physical sense, but what it was they kept us moving around the world and what we might accomplish from it.

When I started writing this book, I sent the first few chapters to an actor friend of mine who was also a gifted writer and asked him to critique it. He had also read the first book I wrote, which detailed our experience in getting Yolande deported inadvertently and our subsequent adventures in Europe while trying to restore her legal status in the U.S. He told me that he had enjoyed the first book but also said that it was simply a narrative of the places we had been and the events that took place along the way. He thought this book had the potential to be something more.

"You're not really writing this book to tell about the places you've been," he told me. "You're writing this book to find out why you go to these places to begin with!"

I thought that the reasons why we went to these places were self-explanatory. My wife and I both enjoyed traveling and we found out that teaching English or volunteering with a charitable organization in another country was a good way to do this and learn about people in the rest of the world at the same time.

"Yeah, but why do you want to do it?" he continued. "Why is doing this so important to you that you're willing to give up all the things that other people have to have that keeps them from doing something similar?"

Before I could come up with an answer, he came up with one for me. "That's why you're writing this book!" he told me. "You're trying to find out for yourself what makes you tick. By the time you finish it, you'll know."

Hmmmm, I thought. That's pretty deep. I wasn't sure if he was right or not, but I did think there was something to that idea. Why was this the only thing I felt like I could do now and be reasonably happy? I didn't start out that way. My academic degrees were in business and for the first 35 years of my career, I couldn't really see me doing anything else. I suppose I could have eventually taken enough classes to begin a different career, or finally decided to stop making excuses for myself and find a way to become an actor, but deep down I knew I didn't have the guts or determination to make a living doing that. I always thought I had the talent, but in the real world, it doesn't matter what you think, it's what other people think, or what you can make other people think.

When the idea of becoming a foreign English teacher first came up, it was naturally exciting and thrilling to think about the adventures and challenges we would encounter by pursuing this this idea. But that was 4 years ago, before all the misadventures and double crosses in China, Chile and Canada. In each of those cases, we started off completely optimistic and trusting the people we were dealing with, never thinking any of them would try to deceive us. But that's exactly what happened in each case, to some extent, although I will admit that in some cases, it might not have been entirely deliberate.

Still, we had been burned in one way or another on all 3 of our journeys, so what made us think it wouldn't happen again? Were we really just naïve, and therefore worthy of being called "Gullible Travelers", willing to believe anything anybody told us if it was what we wanted to hear?

Maybe so. Maybe we weren't behaving rationally after all. I decided to think about what my friend had asked me. Why were we willing to give up some things that other people had to have in order to pursue our fantasy?

First of all, I had to think about what it was that we had given up. I had to admit, there were several. A permanent home, a house (which for many is the ultimate American dream), financial stability, comfortable transportation, familiar surroundings, identifiable televisions shows, community events, the ability to find libraries with books written in English, or places to buy magazines or newspapers printed in English almost everywhere you go, familiar and favorite foods, an understanding of governmental processes and procedures, quick access to effective medical care, the best places to go for any type of food, clothes or other commodity, and probably most important of all, the closeness of relatives and friends.

I thought about all of these comforts which we had forfeited in order to continue our adventures and concluded that the only one which I truly missed was the last one. Yes, of course, I longed for being able to jump in my car and go to a ball game, or a movie or just stop at a local greasy spoon for a hot dog or hamburger made just the way I like it. And I still missed being able to watch almost any professional football or baseball game played by American teams, and also being able to find a book at a local library or a newspaper or magazine I enjoyed reading at a local convenience store, etc, etc., etc., but I realized that a lot of these things can be done online nowadays, and the ones that weren't were usually all replaceable.

All but one. Having family and friends close by and being able to see them on a regular basis. That's the one thing I really missed by having a traveling lifestyle. When you're younger, it isn't that important, but as you get older it becomes more difficult to lose contact with your relatives or longtime friends. Like many things in life, it's something most of us take for granted until it's gone.

So, okay, I didn't get the support I wanted from my family and friends, simply because it was difficult to contact them at times, and often it was just more practical to converse via emails along with an occasional Skype call. But even then, it couldn't replace the bond formed with personal visits and by doing things and going places together.

Maybe it was a little easier for me and Yolande to give up this benefit because neither of us came from large, close-knit families. I was an only child whose parents had passed away many years ago, and the only close relatives I had remaining in the world were my two daughters and an elderly aunt in a nursing home. My aunt was well past the point where she tried to maintain contacts with anyone, and my daughters were scattered thousands of miles apart from each other in America. Due to the time differences between us, we rarely spoke to each other on the phone, except for special occasions. Even when my younger daughter and I lived an hour and a half away from each other in California, we almost never saw each other outside of national holidays. Part of this was because our work schedules were complete opposites – I worked a regular day job Monday through Friday, while she worked nights and weekends which made personal visits difficult any other time. Similarly my older daughter had moved to another state years earlier and she also had an unpredictable schedule which made planning telephone conversations challenging.

Yo on the other hand, had 3 sisters and a brother, but once she left Holland in her early twenties, the rest of the family more or less excluded her from anything family related. Their philosophy seemed to be "out of sight, out of mind" for some reason. It didn't make sense to me but Yo told me that that's just the way they were and nothing we could say or do would ever change it. So neither one of us had the close family ties, or "roots" that a lot of other people had to keep them planted more or less in one particular place. Therefore we didn't have much to lose in this respect by adopting a nomadic lifestyle.

So, in a way, I guess being able to travel and meet new friends and co-workers may have been our way of making up for the "loss" of a close personal relationship with our family and friends. In addition, it gave us the ability to experience life outside of our own borders by learning to live "like the locals" to some extent in each new place we visited. Whereas other people we knew seemed to measure success by the size of their homes, the prestige of their automobiles or jewelry and the size of their bank accounts, Yo and I felt that success meant being happy with your job, or at least satisfied with your mission in life.

But then, after all the deceptions and disappointments we experienced in our trips to China, Chile and Canada, why would we want to gamble with our futures again and trust the promises of people we barely knew?

I think it was because, no matter how upsetting or aggravating these detours on our journeys might have seemed at the time, we both knew deep down that they were nothing compared to the hardships Rieke had gone through, and millions of other people had gone through before her. In short, no matter how bad things might go on one our trips, we were still living a life that was far, far better than the vast majority of people in this world. If having to scrounge for a place to stay, or wait for weeks or months to get paid, or being forced to terminate a project prematurely were the worst things that could happen to us, then we were truly among the luckiest people in the world. And since we were so lucky, why not try to make the most of our existence in this world by expanding our horizons and helping others at the same time.

So the bottom line was we had little or nothing to lose and everything to gain. That was the reason why we did what we did and would continue to do so for a long, long time. We were both in a unique position to help others with minimal cost to ourselves while enjoying the ability to experience new culture and make new friends along the way.

We had found a great way to try to be happy without losing much, if anything in the process, without harming or taking anything away from anyone else, and perhaps possibly helping them find their own happiness in their lives. It was all really pretty simple when I thought about it, but being able to articulate it was something different. But that was the answer. That had to be exactly why we did what we did.

Last but not least, the experience of helping care for Yolande's mom during the last 5 months of her life also taught us a valuable lesson. On the surface, she didn't immediately strike one as an amazing individual. But after learning how she survived the terrors of the Japanese prison camp and somehow found the resiliency to bounce back and lead a meaningful, productive life, it was obvious that almost any hardship can be overcome if one has the will to do it.

So, I guess Yo and I will continue to try to make a contribution to this world while enriching our own lives at the same time, whether it comes in the form of teaching English, performing volunteer work or anything else which helps other people reach their goals. It's not going to change the world on an overall basis, but it might just help make a difference, one person at a time. And as long as we survive our journeys, we will continue to believe the good will outweigh the bad.

I can see how some people might think we're being incredibly naïve to believe that everything will work out for the best, given some of our past experiences, but we're willing to take the risk. We'll continue to believe that there will be more good days than bad wherever we go, more positives than negatives, more good hearted people in the world than bad. In that respect, I guess you could say that we'll always be "Gullible Travelers". At least I hope so.

"The road is long,
There are mountains in our way,
But we climb a step every day"

-Jack Nitszche, Buffy Sainte-Marie,
Will Jennings
Up Where We Belong